The Montana Gardener's Companion

Gardener's Companion Series

The Montana Gardener's Companion

*An Insider's Guide to
Gardening under the Big Sky*

Bob Gough
and Cheryl Moore-Gough

The Globe Pequot Press

GUILFORD, CONNECTICUT
AN IMPRINT OF ROWMAN & LITTLEFIELD

The information in this book has been carefully researched. The author and publisher assume no responsibility for accidents happening to, injuries sustained, or any damage, loss, or inconvenience incurred by the reader as a result of following the information in this book. When using any commercial product, always read and follow label directions. Mention of a trade name does not imply endorsement by the publisher.

Library of Congress Cataloging-in-Publication Data is available.
ISBN: 978-0-7627-4454-1

First Edition/Second Printing

For our sons and daughters and their families

Contents

Introduction viii

Firm Foundations

1. Soil 2

2. Climate 29

3. Water Relations 42

Green Things

4. Lawns 56

5. Vegetables 72

6. Fruit 94

7. Annual Flowers 112

8. Herbaceous Perennials, Bulbs, and Roses 120

9. Trees and Shrubs 135

10. Native Plants 151

Garden Solutions

11. Pests and Problems 164

12. Resources for the Montana Gardener 185

Glossary 199

Index 207

About the Authors 214

Introduction

For years hundreds of gardeners new to the state and frustrated with books that do not pertain to Montana have pleaded with us to write a book specifically on Montana gardening. Here it is.

Montana is the fourth-largest U.S. state in area and, as such, has great variations in soil and climate. Plants that thrive in the western part of the state may die outright in the eastern part. While we are harvesting our first beans in early August in Bozeman, Philipsburg has had its first frost. You've got to be a good gardener to have any success whatsoever in our great state.

It was not our intention to write a comprehensive book on general gardening. There are far too many of those on the market today. Rather, this book presents the basics of gardening *as they are interpreted in Montana*. Many general recommendations do not apply under Montana conditions and can damage or kill your plants. Even recommendations given in books on gardening in the "Rocky Mountains" do not pertain to our entire state, the western parts of which lie in the Northern Rockies while the eastern parts lie in the Northern Great Plains. So *The Montana Gardener's Companion* gives pointers specifically useful to Montana gardeners in every part of the state, and it includes references, resources, and a glossary to help you get more information on Montana gardening.

For precision and convenience, we refer to all but the most common plants by both their common name and their scientific name, since most plants have many common names but only one generally recognized scientific name. *Hortus Third* is our source for plant names. For example, while we all know what a "cucumber" is, the common name "cedar," can refer to plants in the genus *Cedrus* (the true cedars, which do not grow in Montana), *Thuja, Juniperus*, and *Chamaecyparis*. When people call us with a question on their "cedar," we don't know to which plant they refer. Usually, neither do they.

Nymphaea alba is known across Europe by 245 common names, the European white water lily being only one of them. Many of the species of stone fruit in the genus *Prunus* have similar soil and water requirements, so we may refer to them in a shorthand sort of way simply as "*Prunus* spp." (The plural abbreviation for species is "spp."; "sp." is the singular abbreviation.) Where there is a chance the reader will confuse the plant in question, we have supplied the scientific name as well as the common name. The term "cultivar," abbreviated "cv.," means "cultivated variety" and is commonly equivalent to what most of us call "variety." For example, we call 'Jetstar' tomato a "variety" when technically it is a "cultivar." Regardless of what you call it, it's a great indeterminate tomato for the warmer areas of Montana. We use both "cultivar" and "variety" interchangeably in this book.

To prepare this Gardener's Companion, we have gathered our information from Montana research reports, Montana extension publications, and the results of our own research and service over a combined seven decades of gardening activity. Nowhere else will you find so much information specific to Montana gardening. Use a good basic gardening book for fundamental knowledge of how plants grow, then use this book to see what they need to grow in Montana. We hope you enjoy this book as much as you enjoy our alpenglow, our world-class trout fishing, and our gritty rodeos.

Firm
Foundations

C H A P T E R O N E

Soil

All gardening begins with the soil. Healthy soil produces a healthy crop. Healthy soil is dynamic, never static, its components always changing.

The ideal soil is made of about 45 percent minerals, 5 percent organic matter, and 50 percent pore space. About half the pore space is filled with water and half with air. But few Montanans have soil that is ideal both in composition and depth. Inadequate soil depth may limit rooting and hence interfere with plant growth. In general, trees and shrubs do well in soil at least 3 to 4 feet deep. Herbaceous perennials, vines, and larger vegetables like tomatoes and corn need at least 12 inches of good soil. Turfgrass and smaller vegetables like lettuce and radishes should have at least 6 inches of good soil for healthy development.

What kind of soil do you have? How can you improve it? Before you can amend your soil, you need to know what you have to work with. You'll learn about both in this chapter.

Montana has a great variety of soils. Along the Idaho border lies a narrow region of Andisols, fairly productive young soils, gently to steeply sloping, and composed of clays and volcanic material. Directly to the east is a band of Alfisols, moist, generally steep, and originally wooded. These are areas of clay accumulation and mild acidity. The Mollisols spread over much of the central portion of the state and the entire High Line area east of the Continental Divide. These brown soils, most of which originated under prairie conditions, range from dry to moist and can undergo long, intermittent dry periods in summer. Mollisols are highly productive, retain good crumbly surface structure, and do not harden when dry. Much of the central eastern to southeastern parts of Montana are covered with Entisols—young, shallow, hard-to-work soils. They have a high mineral content and low organic matter and range from highly productive to very poorly productive.

There is another type of soil that the master gardeners in Great Falls and much of the eastern part of Montana must contend with—gumbo soil. This nontechnical term refers specifically to soils that have high silt or, more commonly in our state, high clay content. They become sticky and hard to work when wet and hard and impossible to work when dry. They can, however, be quite productive after amendments to improve drainage. "Gumbo," like so many other common terms, is also used by frustrated gardeners in a general sense to refer to any soil that is difficult to work, be it due to high silt or high clay content or to sodic or other conditions. Additions of large amounts of organic matter and sometimes coarse sand as well usually improve the workability of gumbo soil.

How can you determine what soil exists in your yard? For starters, soil maps for many of Montana's counties are available from your local county extension office and from the Montana office of the Natural Resources Conservation Service (see chapter 12, "Resources for the Montana Gardener"). Soil tests will also give you detailed information—more about them later in this chapter.

Physical Properties of Soil

Two of the most important properties of soil are texture and structure. Texture refers to the relative percentage of sand, silt, and clay in the soil makeup. Soil texture cannot be changed significantly, but it can be improved by adding soil amendments. The arrangement of these small soil particles into clusters, or peds, determines the structure of the soil. A third important component is the soil organic matter. Let's look at these three components more closely.

Soil texture: Sand, silt, and clay make up the mineral component of the soil and account for most of the soil texture. Soils composed of weathered granite usually contain high amounts of sand and gravel, while those whose parent material is shale contain much clay. Sand particles are between 0.05 and 2.0 mm in diameter (relatively large), which results in large pore spaces between the particles. Because of this, soils with a high percentage of sand drain excessively and become droughty in summer. Particles of silt are smaller (0.002 to 0.05 mm in diameter), meaning smaller pore spaces. Soils with silt hold more water while still being relatively well drained. Clay particles are smallest (less than 0.002 mm in diameter and invisible to the naked eye). Very small pore spaces separate clay particles, which means the soil can hold much water. Clay soils are poorly drained, easily compacted with foot traffic, and resemble concrete when dried.

A soil that is all sand, or all silt, or all clay, is not useful for the gardener. The best garden soils are the loams, which contain roughly equal parts of the three minerals. Within the loams, those that contain about 60 percent sand and 30 percent silt are known as the sandy loams; those with about 60 percent silt and 30 percent sand are the silt loams. These are the best of the best garden soils. A simple soil test performed by a private testing lab is the most accurate method of determining your soil texture.

Soil structure: Decayed organic matter is called humus. Organic chemicals in humus "glue" soil particles together, making small particles into larger ones called aggregates, or peds, that increase soil porosity and aeration, soil water-holding capacity, and resistance to soil crusting. While soil texture is relatively stable and only changes over long periods of time, soil porosity can be improved relatively rapidly by adding organic matter. Continued tillage without the addition of organic materials tends to lower soil porosity, resulting in surface crusting and compaction, poor water infiltration, and the potential for great erosion.

A quick test of the suitability of your soil for a garden is to take a handful of reasonably moist soil, squeeze it in your hand, and then release the pressure. If the soil does not form a ball, it is too sandy; if it forms a ball that will not break when lightly touched, it is too clayey. The best soil should form a ball that breaks apart when lightly touched.

Soil organic matter is the partially decomposed remains of plants and animals. Soil microorganisms use nitrogen as their energy source to break down organic matter and release its nitrogen, phosphorus, potassium, and other nutrients back into the soil for plant use. When most of the bound nutrients have been released, the organic matter is called humus. While not biologically active, humus improves the soil's physical and chemical properties. Humus is dark, fluffy, and resistant to further decay. Its dark color absorbs heat and speeds plant growth in spring and fall. It acts like a sponge, absorbing soil nutrients and water, preventing them from leaching away from the plant, and then releases them to plant roots over time. Some evidence from researchers at Montana State University suggests that humus may inhibit the loss of calcium phosphate, perhaps keeping the phosphorus in fertilizer more readily available to plants. It also increases the availability of some other metal nutrients.

Organic matter in the soil decomposes more rapidly as precipitation, temperature, and aeration increase. Therefore, decomposition is quite high in an irrigated garden in midsummer following spring and fall tillage. The rate of decomposition also varies with the amount of carbon in the organic material. The more carbon, the slower decomposition and the more nitrogen the microorganisms use to break it down. This is expressed in a material's carbon to nitrogen (C:N) ratio (see the sidebar "The C:N Ratios of Some Common Materials").

Materials with C:N ratios of less than 30:1 break down relatively rapidly. Those with a C:N ratio greater than 30:1 require a greater amount of time to break down and require the addition of

The C:N Ratios of Some Common Materials

The following table lists some organic materials commonly used to improve soil. Note that it is not necessary to add nitrogen to materials with carbon to nitrogen (C:N) ratios below about 30:1.

Material	C:N ratio	Amount of nitrogen to add
Corncobs	420:1	1.5 pounds nitrogen per 100 pounds material
Sawdust, wood chips	400:1	1.5 pounds nitrogen per 100 pounds material
Paper	175:1	1 pound nitrogen per 100 pounds material
Strawy manure	80:1	0.75 pound nitrogen per 100 pounds material
Straw, leaves	75:1	0.75 pound nitrogen per 100 pounds material
Peat moss, corn stalks	60:1	0.5 pound nitrogen per 100 pounds corn stalks; none for peat moss
Horse manure, green rye, and wheat	35:1	Sprinkle of nitrogen per 100 pounds material
Mature sweet clover	24:1	None
Composted manure	20:1	None
Buckwheat	19:1	None
Sheep, poultry manure	15:1	None
Alfalfa hay, normal soil, vegetable waste, clover hay	12:1	None
Raw municipal wastewater	6:1	None
Blood meal	4:1	None

nitrogen-containing fertilizers to speed decomposition. The fertilizer is mixed with the organic matter. Because organic matter continues to break down, therefore, we must add it to the garden on a regular basis to keep the supply of humus where it ought to be. Historically Montana soil organic matter content was estimated to be about 4 percent; today it ranges in many Montana topsoils from 1 percent to 4 percent.

How to Increase Soil Organic Matter

There are several ways you can increase your soil's organic matter. In annual gardens, such as the vegetable garden, turning under green manure crops and cover crops works well.

Green manure crops are grown in the summer on a non-cropped area of the garden and turned under while still green. Crops such as buckwheat, sown at the rate of 2 pounds of seed per 1,000 square feet, and sweet clover, sown at 0.1 pound of seed per 1,000 square feet, make good green manure crops. Both have C:N ratios of about 19:1.

Cover crops are typically sown for winter. While their primary purpose is to hold soil against erosion, they do add good amounts of organic matter when plowed under in spring.

Many Montana soils can benefit from an application of organic material such as manure and compost at a rate of

Cover Crops to Avoid

Don't plant a cover crop of winter rye in Montana! This plant can overwinter and become a terrible volunteer pest in wheat fields. Instead, consider sowing spring oats or sow winter wheat in early autumn. Both will have a C:N ratio of about 60:1 when plowed down, however, so you should add some extra nitrogen at that time to compensate for the amount used in decomposition.

3 to 4 cubic yards per 1,000 square feet. In both your annual and perennial gardens, manure and compost are useful for building the soil organic matter.

Manure. All manure is not equal. Fresh manure adds more nutrients and beneficial organisms than rotted (composted) manure, but it also adds more weed seeds and can burn tender foliage. If you must add fresh manure, plow it into the soil in the autumn when the garden is done and other plants are entering dormancy. For spring feeding, add rotted manure only. The quality of the manure depends upon the species of animal, what the animal ate, how much bedding is contained in the manure, and how the manure was handled before spreading. High amounts of bedding increase the C:N ratio and may mean you'll have to add extra nitrogen to the soil. Manure piled in exposed areas will have much of the nutrient content leached.

Horse manure seems to contain more weed seeds than other manures. Sheep and poultry manure contain much nitrogen and can cause excessive growth. Do not use pet manures or manures of any carnivore since they have the potential to carry parasites. *Note:* One bushel of manure weighs about fifty pounds. Fresh manures are relatively low in phosphorus, so add about two pounds of phosphorus per 1,000 square feet to make up for that. Get that amount from ten pounds of 0-20-0 or fifteen pounds of steamed bonemeal.

Compost. Adding compost is another good way to increase soil organic matter, but generating compost is a long-term investment in Montana. Our dry, cold conditions slow decomposition, and it may take a year or two to make good compost. The finer the raw material, the faster it decomposes, so try to shred everything before you add it to the compost pile.

Compost is a wonderful amendment, but it has no magical qualities. It is simply organic matter decomposed before being added to the garden, resulting in less drain on soil nitrogen. You can use most anything in the compost pile with a few exceptions. Do not compost large bones, grease, meat, eggs and dairy products, or pet manures, as they may attract wildlife. Avoid using grass clippings from a lawn treated with herbicide. Some herbicides may linger for months or years in the clippings and can damage your garden crops. Don't compost walnut leaves because they contain a substance that can be toxic to some plants. If you live in bear country, *do not* place fruit in the compost pile.

To make a compost bin, use 2-by-4-inch mesh welded wire and form it into a circle or attach it to stakes. Put the bin near the garden. Place a 6-inch-deep layer of organic material at the bottom, sprinkle it with a nitrogen-containing fertilizer mix of your choice, then add a 3-inch-deep layer of soil, manure, or compost over it. Sprinkle with water. Repeat this process until the bin is full.

Composting Fertilizer Recipe

To make your composting fertilizer, mix twenty pounds of a 10 percent nitrogen fertilizer and ten pounds of ground limestone; add one pound of this to every forty pounds of green material. Organic gardeners mix fifteen pounds of wood ash, seven pounds of dried blood, and four pounds of steamed bonemeal and add three pounds of this mix to every forty pounds of green material. Be aware that this organic mix contains animal products and could attract unwanted critters.

The soil and organic material contain all the necessary elements for making good compost; you need not add any fancy store-bought products containing enzymes to get the compost pile cooking. Keep the top of the pile flat or concave and covered with a tarp to prevent excessive moisture loss. Sprinkle it as needed to keep the material moist. Turn the pile every six weeks or so, or when the temperature begins to decline, moving material from the outside and the top of the pile into the middle. Material at the center of a good working pile will heat to about 130 degrees

Fahrenheit, killing many pathogens and weed seeds. The compost will be ready when the material has broken down and become a crumbly, deep brown product bearing no resemblance to the original material.

Chemical Properties of Montana Soil

Soil fertility is intertwined with its physical and chemical properties. Knowing your soil pH, for example, helps you to know what nutrients are most likely to be available in abundance or completely unavailable.

The pH of the soil is an expression of its acidity, neutrality, or alkalinity. On a scale of 1 to 14, a pH of 7 is neutral. Higher numbers indicate increasing alkalinity; lower numbers indicate increasing acidity. For comparison, stomach acid and lemon juice are about pH 2, coffee about 3.5, orange juice 4, milk 6, seawater about 8.5, soap 9, bleach about 12.5, and lye (sodium hydroxide) about 14. Pure water is 7 (neutral).

Since the pH scale is logarithmic, there is a difference of a factor of ten between numbers. For example, a soil pH of 5 is ten times more acid than a pH of 6 and one hundred times more acid (ten times ten) than a pH of 7.

The acidity or alkalinity of the soil regulates the decomposition of organic matter, the action of some pesticides, and the availability of nutrients to the plant. For example, there may be plenty of iron in the soil, but a high pH binds that iron and makes it unavailable to many plants. That is why you need to know the pH of your soil and to amend it accordingly for best plant growth.

Most of our garden plants grow best at soil pHs of 6 to 7 because that is the range in which nutrients are highly available to plants. Soil microorganisms that break down organic material and increase nutrient availability are also most active in a near-neutral soil.

Some garden plants will tolerate a soil pH above 7.5, but few

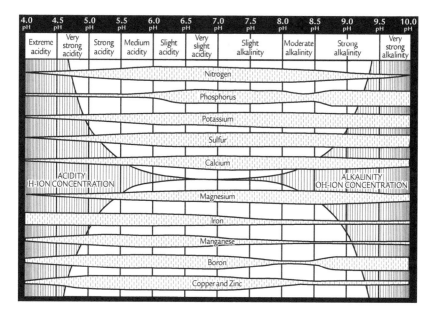

4.0 pH	4.5 pH	5.0 pH	5.5 pH	6.0 pH	6.5 pH	7.0 pH	7.5 pH	8.0 pH	8.5 pH	9.0 pH	9.5 pH	10.0 pH
Extreme acidity	Very strong acidity	Strong acidity	Medium acidity	Slight acidity	Very slight acidity		Slight alkalinity	Moderate alkalinity		Strong alkalinity		Very strong alkalinity

Nitrogen
Phosphorus
Potassium
Sulfur
Calcium
ACIDITY H-ION CONCENTRATION
ALKALINITY OH-ION CONCENTRATION
Magnesium
Iron
Manganese
Boron
Copper and Zinc

Soil pH and Nutrient Availability

thrive at that range. On the other hand, ericaceous plants like rhododendrons, azaleas, and blueberry do best at a decidedly acidic pH 5; try to grow them at a soil pH above 6 and they will show an iron deficiency. (That is the reason ericaceous plants generally are not recommended for Montana.) If your soil pH is way out of whack, you will have to modify it for the best garden plant growth.

The pH of most Montana soils is neutral to alkaline (pH 7 to 8) but can vary on specific

pH for Potatoes

Agriculturists recommend a soil pH of about 5.5 for potatoes because at that pH the microorganism that causes potato scab becomes inactive and infection rates are low. While the potato plant will grow just as well at pH 7, the scab organism will grow better. Potatoes grown on alkaline soils have more problems with potato scab infections than spuds grown in acidic soils.

sites from a very acidic pH 4.5 to a strongly alkaline pH 8.5. In general, areas in the eastern part of the state at lower elevations and with less precipitation tend to have higher pHs since the base-forming elements like calcium cannot be leached. Areas in the western part of the state at higher elevations and receiving greater precipitation tend to have lower pHs. These are soils formed from acid parent material, forest soils, and mining sites containing iron and sulfur.

Let's look at common Montana soils and how to adjust them for the best gardens.

Alkaline Soils

Alkaline soils tend to be high in calcium, magnesium, and potassium and, if the pH is above 7.4, low in manganese, iron, and boron. Most soils in Montana are alkaline. It is difficult to lower a Montana soil's pH due to our soils' resistance to change (known as the buffering capacity). Add plenty of organic matter, use acid fertilizers like ammonium sulfate (21-0-0) and the ammonium phosphates (11-52-0 and 18-46-0), and improve the soil drainage. Even so, lowering pH is not that simple. Some organic matter, such as some manures, may actually be alkaline. Montana researchers have found that constant annual tillage, as you would practice in the garden, may counteract acidifying agents and in itself raise soil pH. Applying elemental sulfur will help to lower the soil pH. How much you must add depends upon soil type and upon how much you must lower the pH, but in general, about forty pounds of sulfur per 1,000 square feet on a loamy soil will lower the pH from 8.0 to about 6.5. Nevertheless, given the soils' buffering capacity, the pH will rise rapidly so that the addition of sulfur and other acid-forming materials will be an annual chore. Use agricultural sulfur, also called prilled sulfur, and not the flowers of sulfur found in pharmacies. The latter will not dissolve well in water.

Acid Soils

Soils below pH 6 may be deficient in potassium, calcium, and magnesium and may make phosphorus unavailable to plants. At very low pHs, aluminum, boron, zinc, iron, and manganese become highly soluble and can become toxic to the plant. Fortunately, we don't have much of that in Montana, where too high a pH is usually the problem. While acid soils are rarely encountered in Montana, some soils in the mountains and near Great Falls have a pH around 5. To raise the soil pH, apply about 100 pounds of ground limestone per 1,000 square feet or about 300 pounds of wood ash to the same area. Wood ash contains about 6 percent potash and 2 percent phosphorus as well as calcium. Since wood ash may contain some heavy metals, limit your application rate to about one five-gallon bucket of ash per 1,000 square feet per season. The precise amount of material you add depends upon soil type and how much you need to alter the pH. Determine this with a soil test.

Salty Soils

Large parts of Montana once lay at the bottom of an inland sea; the water evaporated and the salt remained. Arid areas, especially in eastern Montana, are particularly impacted by salty soils, but they can also occur throughout the state in low-lying "saline seeps." These are especially plentiful in areas west and northwest of Great Falls east of the Divide and in the far northeastern portions of Sheridan County.

"Saline" soils especially common in eastern and central Montana contain high amounts of carbonate, chloride, and sulfate salts of calcium, magnesium, and potassium that often form white crusts on the soil's surface. These excess salts make it difficult for plants to extract water from the soil and, at high concentrations, actually pull water out of the plant roots. Plant toxicity symptoms include a burning of the leaf edges, wilting, stunting, and poor germination.

"Sodic" soils contain large amounts of sodium salts and often have pHs above 8.5. The sodium causes soil particles to disperse, just as dish soap causes a grease slick to disperse. The result is smaller pore spaces and easily compacted soil. When the soil is wet, the water puddles on the surface; when it is dry, it becomes cementlike. Sometimes a black crust forms on the surface of sodic soils, the result of dispersed organic matter.

"Saline-sodic" soils are those having both excess salt and excess sodium. They display characteristics intermediate between those of sodic and saline soils.

Managing salty soils can be difficult. Some manures and fertilizers contribute to the accumulation of salts in the soil, so avoid the overuse of commercial fertilizers and avoid manure from feedlots. Continue to incorporate good amounts of organic matter, especially straw, into the soil annually where possible and avoid the use of salty irrigation water, including "softened" water. If good water is available, sprinkling about 10 inches of water (about 6,230 gallons per 1,000 square feet) on your soil will remove about 75 percent of the salts in the upper 12 inches of soil.

Sodic soils are particularly troublesome and difficult to work. Enter gypsum! Gypsum (calcium sulfate) often is recommended to lower soil pH, but it will not do so. But it *does* help to leach salts when the calcium in the gypsum replaces the sodium in the soil. Incorporate fine gypsum (60 mesh) into the soil and water well, leaching as much sodium as possible. The right amount of gypsum depends upon the sodium content of the soil.

If you have a saline-sodic soil, amend for the sodic portion first, then work on the saline portion.

Boron (B) can become toxic in saline irrigation water. Symptoms in plants appear first as yellowing, spotting, or drying of the leaf margins and tips. Woody ornamentals and fruit crops are sensitive to boron toxicity. Some plants can handle excess soil boron better than others (see the sidebar "Plant Tolerance to Boron").

Plant salt-tolerant plants if you have salty soil. The following is a partial list of plants, drawn from MSU Extension Bulletin EB 123 (see chapter 12), that will tolerate these conditions in Montana. Remember, when selecting any species for the landscape, you must consider ambient conditions other than saline

Field Signs of Saline Soil

Look to the signs in the field first to see if you have a salinity problem; rely on soil tests second. These field signs include the following characteristics:

- Permanent or seasonal high water table in semiarid regions.

- Thick, continuous crusts form in saline seeps.

- Thin, patchy salt crusts form under clods or on the shady side of clods in marginal areas.

- Poor, spotty stand establishment of grass or crops may indicate poor germination caused by high salts.

- Herbaceous crops appear blue green under salt stress.

- Leaf tip burn and die-off of older leaves in grains can be the result of salt stress or drought stress.

Plant Tolerance to Boron

Tolerant to excess boron	Semitolerant to excess boron	Sensitive to excess boron
Asparagus	Bell pepper	Apple
Beets	Corn	Apricot
Cabbage	Nuts	Cherry
Carrot	Potato	Grape
Gladiolus	Pumpkin	Jerusalem artichoke
Lettuce	Sunflower	Peach
Onion	Sweet pea	Pear
Turnip	Tomato	Plum
	Zinnia	Walnut

soils, such as pH, wind, precipitation, and chinooks. (We'll discuss these in chapter 2.) Not all species listed below do well in all areas of Montana. An asterisk indicates plants that do better in moist, salty soil. The others better tolerate dry, salty soils.

Deciduous Trees and Shrubs for Saline Soils

Best
Norway maple (*Acer platanoides*)
Horse chestnut (*Aesculus hippocastanum*)
Green ash (*Fraxinus pennsylvanica* var. *lanceolata*)
Honey locust (*Gleditsia tricanthos*)
White poplar (*Populus alba*)
Cottonwood (*Populus deltoides*)
Black locust (*Robinia pseudoacacia*)
Juneberry (*Amelanchier canadensis*)
Sagebrush (*Artemesia* spp.)
Caragana (*Caragana arborescens*)

*Curlleaf mountain mahogany (*Cercocarpus ledifolius*)
Chokecherry (*Prunus virginiana*)
*Skunkbush sumac (*Rhus trilobata*)
Staghorn sumac (*Rhus typhina*)
*Sage (*Salvia* spp.)

Good
Box elder (*Acer negundo*)
Birch (*Betula papyrifera, B. pendula*)
Catalpa (*Catalpa speciosa*)
Apple (*Malus* spp.)
Lombardy poplar (*Populus nigra* 'Italica')
Quaking aspen (*Populus tremuloides*)
Ussurian pear (*Pyrus ussuriensis*)
European mountain ash (*Sorbus aucuparia*)
American elm (*Ulmus americana*)
Burningbush (*Euonymus alatus*)
Honeysuckle (*Lonicera* spp.)
Buckthorn (*Rhamnus* spp.)
Japanese tree lilac (*Syringa reticulata*)
Common lilac (*Syringa vulgaris*)
*Buffaloberry (*Sherpherdia argentea*)

Evergreens for Saline Soils

Best
Jack pine (*Pinus banksiana*)
*White spruce (*Picea glauca*)
*Mugo pine (*Pinus mugo*)
Austrian pine (*Pinus nigra*)
*Colorado spruce (*Picea pungens*)
Junipers (*Juniperus* spp.)

Good
Rocky Mountain juniper (*Juniperus scopulorum*)
Norway spruce (*Picea abies*)
Ponderosa pine (*Pinus ponderosa*)

Scots pine (*Pinus sylvestris*)
Douglas fir (*Pseudotsuga menziesii*)
Yew (*Taxus* spp.)
*Arborvitae (*Thuja occidentalis*)
*Hemlock (*Tsuga canadensis*)
*Soapweed (*Yucca glauca*)

Soil Fertility

You may find specialty fertilizers on the store shelf that claim to contain "fifty elements from the sea" with the suggestion that the product will produce super-duper garden plants. Nonsense. There are seventeen elements essential for plant growth. All others are superfluous. These seventeen are subdivided into macronutrients and micronutrients based on plant needs, not on the amounts absorbed. Macronutrients are needed in greater quantities than the micronutrients.

All nutrients must be dissolved in water before the plant can absorb them. If there is a lack of water, your plants may begin to show signs of nutrient deficiencies when in fact there is no real deficiency in the soil at all.

Macronutrients

About 90 percent of a plant is made of carbon, hydrogen, and oxygen extracted from air and water. Because of their ubiquitous sources, these nutrients are never deficient. Carbon (C) makes up the sugars and cellulose in the plant and is necessary for photosynthesis. Hydrogen (H) is an important element in biochemical reactions and a component of carbohydrates. Oxygen (O), also a component of carbohydrates, is necessary for respiration and plant growth.

Nitrogen, phosphorus, and potassium are the primary macronutrients; calcium, magnesium, and sulfur the secondary macronutrients.

Nitrogen (N) strongly promotes rapid growth in leaves, roots, and stems and is the nutrient most often lacking in Montana gardens. Leafy plants such as turfgrass, spinach, lettuce, and kale require large amounts for best growth. Some plants have a symbiotic relationship with root-nodule-forming bacteria to supplement their supply of nitrogen. Atmospheric nitrogen cannot be used directly by plants, and these bacteria "fix" the nitrogen into a form in which it can be used to the benefit of the host plant. Legumes like beans, peas, clover, and alfalfa have this association and are particularly valuable in building soil nitrogen when they are grown and turned under as a green manure crop. (An acre of peas can fix about seventy pounds of nitrogen, an acre of beans forty pounds, and an acre of soybeans a bit over fifty pounds.) The nitrogen in organic fertilizers is in too chemically complex a form to be used by plants directly and is broken down by soil microbes into simple nitrate and ammonium forms that *can* be utilized. About half the nitrogen in manure volatilizes into the atmosphere before the plants can use it, and about half the nitrogen in commercial fertilizers is used by microorganisms to decompose soil organic matter and hence cannot be used by the plants.

What are the signs of a nitrogen-deficient condition? The older, bottom leaves of plants turn a golden yellow. Shoot growth and overall plant growth is stunted, leaves are small, and the young shoots become unusually woody.

Phosphorus (P) generally promotes root, flower, fruit, and seed development. Most Montana soils have sufficient phosphorus, but the nutrient is bound tightly and not available for absorption. Phosphorus is relatively immobile in the soil, and so it should be applied in the plant's root zone, where it can be absorbed quickly. With insufficient phosphorus the plant stems will become stubby and thin, growth and maturity will be delayed, and the leaves and young shoots will develop a pinkish color. By the way, there is no evidence at all that phosphorus directly stimulates only root growth. Specialty high-phosphorus "bulb" or "transplant" fertilizers stimulate a vigorous root system no better than other complete fertilizers.

Potassium (K) promotes general vigor and root growth of the plant but readily leaches from the soil if not held in place by sufficient organic matter. Root crops such as parsnips and carrots especially benefit from a good supply of this nutrient. A potassium deficiency causes development of a grayish area near the margins of older leaves, which in time become necrotic (dead). Yellow areas may develop across the remainder of the leaf.

Calcium (Ca) is necessary for building strong plant cells and for holding the cells together. Calcium is rarely deficient in Montana soils, but drought may make it difficult for plants to absorb this nutrient. A deficiency causes blossom end rot of tomato, bitter pit of apple, tip burn in cabbage, internal browning in brussels sprouts, and cavity spot in parsnips. Excess amounts of potassium can sometimes induce a calcium deficiency. That's why grass clippings high in potassium from a heavily fertilized lawn should not be used to mulch apple trees, as the clippings may induce a calcium deficiency and its resulting spotty fruit.

Magnesium (Mg) is needed for chlorophyll production. It is usually not deficient in our soils. However, a deficiency might occur in sandy soils, which allow the nutrient to be leached from the root zone, or in soils with an overabundance of calcium or potassium. A magnesium deficiency shows as interveinal chlorosis (yellow between the veins) and as premature dropping of older leaves. Since magnesium is not often deficient in Montana soils, there is little merit for the wholesale application of Epsom salts (magnesium sulfate) to rosebushes in Montana to increase bloom.

Sulfur (S) deficiency is becoming relatively more common in Montana due to the lower sulfur content of modern fertilizers, the reduction in sulfur dioxide emissions from burning fossil fuels, and the increased removal of sulfur from soil by high-yield crops. The nutrient is necessary to manufacture some proteins in the plant and contributes pungency to onions, garlic, turnips, and radishes and the characteristic smell to cooked cabbage. Garlic fertilized with high-sulfur fertilizers becomes more pungent.

Micronutrients

Deficiencies of these nutrients, except for iron, are relatively uncommon in Montana. Sandy soils, soils low in organic matter, and strongly alkaline soils may contribute to some deficiencies. Unlike the macronutrients, there is a very fine line between deficiency and toxicity of micronutrients. Do not add these to the soil unless you are absolutely sure of a certain deficiency.

Iron (Fe) is the micronutrient most often limiting in Montana. While there is sufficient iron in our soil, iron is unavailable for plant use in alkaline conditions. The nutrient may also become deficient in waterlogged soils and soils very low in organic matter. Your plants need this nutrient for chlorophyll synthesis and for use in some other biochemical reactions. Iron deficiency shows as an interveinal chlorosis in the youngest leaves, appearing as a bright canary yellow. Certain plants are particularly susceptible to this deficiency in Montana, including ginnala maple, raspberry, roses, apple, and mountain ash.

Zinc (Zn) is needed as part of the enzyme system in plants. Like iron it becomes less available as the soil pH increases and can be deficient in soils with very high organic matter or very high phosphorus content. Some deficiencies have been noted in sugar beets and beans in the lower Yellowstone River valley, but in general the nutrient is rarely limited in Montana.

Boron (B) may be deficient in some areas of the state, especially where high levels of soil potassium exist. Necessary for carbohydrate metabolism, its lack results in sunken, black pithy spots in the fruit and stems of celery, beets, turnips, and apples. The stems of celery and other crucifers will be hollow and cracked. Pollination and fruit set diminish.

Copper (Cu) is involved in proper enzyme function and can become deficient where very high C:N organic material has been turned under and in sandy soils.

Molybdenum (Mo) facilitates nitrogen fixation in legumes and is rarely deficient in Montana.

Chlorine (Cl) is needed for photosynthesis. It is deficient in some soils in Montana where there are very low natural levels of the nutrient or where the soil traditionally has received little potassium fertilization. Since it leaches readily, plants in areas of the state receiving relatively high precipitation can show a deficiency, although wheat and durum wheat are the only crops in the state to have displayed a confirmed chlorine deficiency.

Manganese (Mn) is also involved in proper enzyme function but is rarely deficient in Montana.

Nickel (Ni) is needed in enzyme function and seed germination. This nutrient was added to the list of essential nutrients only in 1987, so we know very little about deficiencies and factors governing its availability.

Soil Sampling and Soil Tests

Although nitrogen is the element most often lacking in our soils, it's a good idea to have your soil tested periodically to see what else may be limited. Soil tests are useful for lawns, annual and perennial beds, and vegetable gardens. They are not very useful in predicting the needs of woody plants in the landscape.

Here's how to do your soil sampling: In late fall (for spring planting) and in late summer (for fall planting), select several sites throughout your yard and garden. Remove organic matter such as sod, leaves, and so on from them. Then, using a spade or garden trowel, collect about a cup of soil from the upper 6 to 8 inches at each site. Mix the soil samples in a clean bucket and gather one cup of the composite mixture for analysis.

Take separate samples from particular trouble spots. Store the soil samples at 40 degrees or dry them soon after collection, and place them in a plastic bag or in the container provided by the testing laboratory. There may be great variability in accuracy and in fertilizer recommendations among laboratories, so find a laboratory you like and stick with it. See chapter 12 for a list of soil testing labs and interpretive literature, or contact your local MSU county extension office for more information.

Fertilizers

With your test results in hand, it's time to decide the kind and amount of fertilizer that is right for your garden. You may use a commercial or an organic fertilizer. The choice is yours. Each has its good and bad points. The nutrients in commercial fertilizers are more concentrated, easy to handle, have no odor, and are readily available to plants. Commercial fertilizers are easily procured and come in many forms, but none of them contain organic matter. Organic fertilizers do contain valuable organic matter but may be difficult to procure, are not easily handled, and usually emit some odors. Their nutrients are not highly concentrated and become available only through microbial action. (Refer to the "Popular Organic Fertilizers" sidebar.)

Concentrated commercial fertilizers are used in small quantities. Some have names, such as ammonium sulfate (see the "Popular Commercial Fertilizers" sidebar), but many are known only by the three numbers appearing on the label. These numbers are called the "analysis" and refer to the percentages of nitrogen and the oxides of phosphorus and potassium the fertilizers contain. For example, 10-10-10 fertilizer contains 10 percent nitrogen and 10 percent each of the oxides. For simplicity we say that it contains 10 percent nitrogen (N), 10 percent phosphorus (P), and 10 percent potassium (K). If you wish you may convert the oxide of phosphorus to elemental phosphorus by multiplying it by 0.44. Do the same with potassium by multiplying the oxide by 0.83. Therefore, a bag of 10-10-10 really contains 10 percent nitrogen, 4.4 percent phosphorus, and 8.3 percent potassium.

Popular Organic Fertilizers

The following list shows the proximate analysis for some popular organic fertilizers and the amounts needed to supply one to two pounds of actual nitrogen (N) per 1,000 square feet. This is a common rate of application for trees, shrubs, flowers, vegetables, and lawns.

Amounts of phosphorus (P) and potassium (K) are listed along with the nitrogen.

Blood: 13% N, 0.9% P, 0.8% K. Apply 10 pounds. Expensive; has odor; attracts predators.

Compost: 2.0% N, 1.0% P, 1.0% K. Apply 4 to 6 inches.

Dehydrated cattle manure: 1.5% N, 2.0% P, 2.3% K. Apply 200 pounds.

Dehydrated chicken manure: 3.5% N, 2.0% P, 2.6% K. Apply 100 pounds.

Dehydrated goat manure: 1.4% N, 1.0% P, 3.0% K. Apply 200 pounds.

Fish meal: 10.0% N, 3.8% P, no K. Apply 15 pounds. N and P are available slowly.

Fresh cattle manure: 0.5% N, 0.2% P, 0.5% K. Apply 500 pounds. Heavy; has odor.

Fresh chicken manure: 1.5% N, 1.0% P, 0.5% K. Apply 300 pounds. Heavy; has odor.

Fresh hog manure: 0.7% N, 0.6% P, 0.7% K. Apply 500 pounds. Heavy; has odor.

Fresh horse manure: 0.7% N, 0.3% P, 0.5% K. Apply 500 pounds. Heavy; has odor.

Fresh rabbit manure: 2.0% N, 1.3% P, 1.2% K. Apply 150 pounds. Heavy; has odor.

Fresh sheep manure: 1.4% N, 0.7% P, 1.5% K. Apply 300 pounds. Heavy; has odor.

Greensand: No nitrogen, 1.0% P, 7.0% K. Apply 150 to 300 pounds. K is slowly available.

Rock phosphate: No nitrogen, 30.0% P, no K. Apply 150 to 300 pounds. Dusty; slowly available.

Steamed bonemeal: 2.0% N, 12.0% P, no K. Apply15 pounds. Expensive.

Popular Commercial Fertilizers

The following table gives the analyses of some concentrated commercial fertilizers commonly used in Montana gardens. "S" refers to sulfur.

Fertilizer	Percent nitrogen	Percent phosphorus oxide	Percent potassium oxide	Notes
Ammonium nitrate	34	0	0	Sales may be restricted
Monoammonium phosphate	11	50	0	1–3% S
Diammonium phosphate	18	46	0	2% S
Ammonium sulfate	21	0	0	24% S
Potassium chloride	0	0	60	
Potassium sulfate	0	0	52	18% S
Urea	46	0	0	
Triple superphosphate	0	50	0	1% S

Single-nutrient fertilizers are blended to create one with a more complete analysis. This eliminates having to buy the nutrients in separate bags and apply them separately. Fertilizers with analyses of 5-10-10, 10-10-10, 16-16-16, 20-20-20, and 27-7-7 are common in Montana in both granular and liquid form and are called "complete fertilizers."

Because the nutrients in fertilizers must be dissolved before the plant can use them, liquid fertilizers are most rapidly available to the plant after application. Granular fertilizers must first be dissolved in rain or irrigation water before their nutrients become available to the plant. This may take a couple of weeks. Organic fertilizers must first be broken down by soil microbes and then their nutrients dissolved before a plant can use them. This makes them the most slowly available of all the common fertilizers.

Determining How Much Fertilizer to Apply

Recommended rates for fertilizer applications will often stipulate the pounds of actual nitrogen required. One pound of actual nitrogen per 1,000 square feet is a common recommendation for lawns, trees, and shrubs; two to three pounds of actual nitrogen per 1,000 square feet for vegetables. You can calculate how much of any given fertilizer you need using the problem and formula below:

Problem:

You wish to apply one pound of actual nitrogen (N) per 1,000 square feet to a 5,000-square-foot lawn using ammonium sulfate with an analysis of 21-0-0.

General Formula:

$$\frac{\text{N application rate (lbs./1000 sq. ft.)}}{\text{N content of fertilizer as a decimal}} \times \frac{\text{plot size (sq. ft.)}}{1000}$$

Formula for Problem:

$$\frac{1.0}{0.21} \times \frac{5000}{1000} = \frac{5}{0.21} = 24 \text{ lbs.}$$

Therefore, you must apply twenty-four pounds of ammonium sulfate to the lawn.

Nutrient Needs Vary

Different types of plants have different nutritional needs. Plants with harvestable parts, such as fruits and vegetables, usually require higher rates of fertility.

In general, vegetables need high amounts of nutrients and are often fertilized several times per season with two to three pounds of actual nitrogen per 1,000 square feet at each application. However, this application rate varies with the vegetable. Herbs, lawns, fruit, and annuals need medium amounts and may be fertilized with about three pounds of actual nitrogen per 1,000 square feet per year. Trees and shrubs need low amounts and often need none at all. Do not fertilize trees and shrubs unless you determine they need it. If they do, apply the fertilizer in late fall after the leaves on deciduous trees turn color.

Here are recommendations for how much fertilizer to apply to woody ornamentals in Montana, as explained in the *Montana Master Gardener Handbook* (see chapter 12).

- Shade trees with trunk diameter (measured 4 feet off the ground) of less than 6 inches: Apply 0.15 to 0.3 pound of nitrogen per inch diameter.

- Trees with trunk diameter greater than 6 inches in diameter: Apply 0.3 to 0.6 pound of nitrogen per inch diameter.

- Shrubs: 0.05 to 0.10 pound nitrogen per foot of height or spread.

When you apply fertilizer, broadcast it over lawns and within the dripline of trees and shrubs and side-dress it in vegetable and flower gardens. Keep all herbicide-containing lawn fertilizers out of plants' driplines. Spray liquid fertilizers onto foliage or on the soil around the plants. The time of application varies with the species and will be addressed in later chapters.

As we said at the beginning of this chapter, few Montanans have ideal soil. But by following the recommendations given here, you have a good shot at creating a good soil—and that can lead to you having a garden or yard that is the envy of your neighbors.

Climate

Montana west of the Continental Divide is composed of mountains and narrow valleys. East of the Divide the land has broad valleys interspersed with isolated mountains, conforming mostly to a Great Plains terrain. The lowest elevation in the state is 1,800 feet at the Canadian border in the state's extreme northwest corner; the highest, 12,850 feet, is at the top of Granite Peak near the state's south-central line with Wyoming. While the mean elevation is 3,400 feet, about half of the state lies above 5,000 feet.

Eastern Montana generally has colder winters, hotter summers, less frequent and less total rainfall, more wind, more sun, and a longer growing season than western Montana and is subject to the famous winter chinooks, when warm air masses slide rapidly down the eastern slope of the Rockies, resulting in temperature changes of as much as 100 degrees Fahrenheit in 24 hours. The cold air that follows chinooks is devastating to plants when those chinooks occur in January and February, just as plants begin to lose their greatest winter hardiness.

Temperatures exceeding 100 degrees can occur in any month from May to September and below zero in any month from September to May. July is typically the only month without snowfall, but the autumns are usually mild and open. With all these climatic challenges it may seem impossible to have a good Montana garden. But by the time you finish this chapter, you'll see that a great garden is not only possible but logical if you keep climate in mind!

Climate and Hardiness Zones

The U.S. Department of Agriculture (USDA) Hardiness Zones were developed by tracking average minimum winter temperatures over decades. A newly revised hardiness map is available at www.arborday.org. Most of Montana lies in Zone 4. Parts of western Montana, with their milder climate, lie in Zone 5, while Zone 3 covers much of the eastern part of the state. Islands of warmer or colder zones lie within larger zones, the results of varying degrees of elevation.

Most gardeners grant the USDA Hardiness Zone maps too high a level of precision. Hardiness zones are relevant only to perennial plants, not annuals, and the zones say nothing about the other factors that influence gardening success—including length of the growing season, soils, wind, salinity, or humidity in an area. Since some winters are warmer and some colder than average, you can see great fluctuations in zone designations from year to year. Our rule of thumb is that any hardiness zone designation is accurate in any given year to plus or minus one full zone. To be on the safe side, always select plants with a hardiness rating one zone lower than that given for your area.

Your Growing Season

Montana's growing season is highly variable and relatively short. Cool nights retard plant growth but are partially offset by the intense sunlight and the long summer days. Elevation, latitude, and longitude all affect your growing season. According to Hopkin's bioclimatic law, spring bloom of a species is delayed by four days as you move up by 400 feet in elevation, or north by 1 degree in latitude above the equator, or east by 5 degrees in lon-

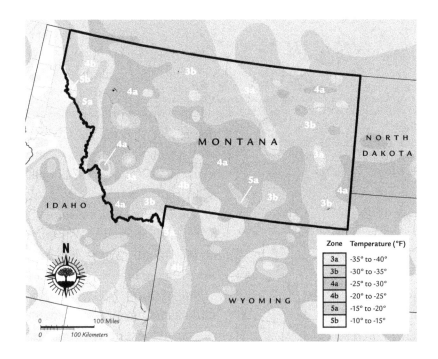

USDA Hardiness Zones for Montana

Zone	Temperature (°F)
3a	-35° to -40°
3b	-30° to -35°
4a	-25° to -30°
4b	-20° to -25°
5a	-15° to -20°
5b	-10° to -15°

gitude. In autumn the season ends four days earlier for every 400 feet in elevation, for every 1 degree of more northerly latitudes, and for every 5 degrees of more westerly longitude.

Growing seasons are not always that mathematically predictable in the garden, where microclimates play an important role. For example, the flower bed on the south side of your house receives sunlight and heat all day year-round, while the flower bed on the east side receives sunlight only in the morning. These differences in environments are called microclimates, and every yard has them. Additionally, the growing season is generally longer in the southeast corner of the state, in the lower valleys, and along the major rivers like the Yellowstone. Spring comes earlier and autumn later at lower elevations. Also, since temperature drops about 1 degree for every 25 feet rise in elevation, the season is far shorter at higher elevations in the western part of the state, where frosts may occur in every month.

Heat does not travel far in our dry air. It may be 90 degrees in the summer sun but 60 degrees in the shade. Mix this with changes in elevation, and that means areas only 6 miles apart can be considerably colder in winter, warmer in summer, and have a difference of as much as one month in the length of the growing season. Montana is a state of microclimates. A good understanding of microclimates can mean the difference between a great garden and no garden at all.

The timing of the bloom of the common purple lilac (*Syringa vulgaris*) is used throughout the nation to determine the advancement of spring. This plant blooms before May 12 in the southeastern counties along the Big Horn River and the Yellowstone River in Big Horn, Yellowstone, and parts of Treasure County, but lilac does not bloom until mid-May in surrounding areas extending north to the Fort Peck Reservoir. By mid- to late May, it has bloomed in most of eastern Montana and in the valleys of western Montana and has completed bloom in nearly all areas of the state. In general, the lilac bloom advances to higher elevations at a rate of about 100 feet per day and, at any given elevation, advances north about 15 miles per day.

In many years Montana gardeners can enjoy extended

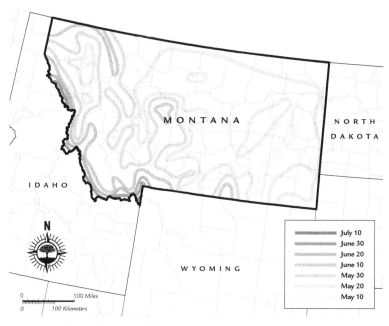

Average date of the last killing frost in Montana. The actual date can
vary by plus or minus two weeks from the average date.

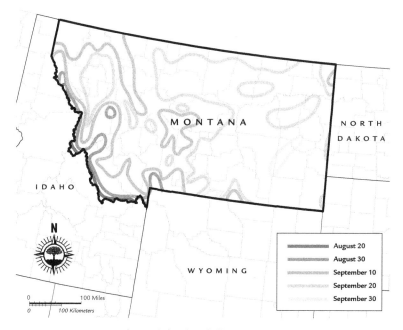

Average date of the first killing frost in Montana.
The actual date can vary by plus or minus two weeks.

Source: USDA Yearbook of Agriculture, 1941.

Generally, not many seeds
germinate or plants grow
when temperatures are
below 45 degrees. Be sure
soil temperatures 2 inches
deep are at least 60
degrees before you plant
annuals and vegetables.
Most plants don't grow
much when the tempera-
ture tops 90 degrees and
suffer greatly in dry soil
when the temperature
exceeds about 95 degrees.

autumns, beginning a few days after a killing frost. Officially the growing season has ended, but if you protect your tomatoes and squash with blankets or sprinklers when frost is predicted, they'll continue to produce crops for a few more weeks. Covers that keep the ground heat near the plant canopy and prevent it from bleeding off into the cold night sky are most effective.

The growing season is conventionally defined as the length of time between last frost in spring and the first frost in fall. This definition is misleading. It is true that plant growth stops at 32 degrees, but even our cold-hardy plants make poor growth at temperatures between 32 and 45 degrees. Above about 90 degrees, cool-season plants—which make up most of the Montana gardener's landscape—make no productive growth at all. For this reason the length of the actual growing season is always shorter than the published length. However, the shorter time is partially compensated by the longer days and the more intense sunlight plants enjoy in Montana. In general, plan for your vegetable plants to take far

Wind-Worthy Plantings

Plants for windy areas include thornless honey locust, with its feathery foliage, and low-growing shrubs such as the junipers.

longer to mature than the number of days to harvest indicated on seed packets. A sixty-three-day sweet corn may take ninety-three days to ripen in Bozeman!

Avoid the temptation to plant too early, for cold, wet soil may rot the seeds. If they do germinate, the strong possibility of a late frost means the chances of a plant's sur-vival are slim. Furthermore, assuming the plants do germinate and escape a late frost, the cold soil slows growth. In every case plants set out or seeds planted safely as much as two weeks later catch up with the earlier planting. In this instance the early bird catches nothing but cold.

Precipitation

The wettest areas of the state may receive 20 inches of annual precipitation, but few areas of the state receive more than about 12 inches during the growing season. All Montana gardens and landscapes must have supplemental irrigation to succeed.

Winter precipitation in the form of snowfall is least in the eastern parts of the state and snow cover is intermittent through most winters. Only at higher elevations will snow cover remain throughout the winter months. A continual snow cover insulates plants from extreme cold and adds to the soil water profile as it melts in spring.

Irrigation must be more frequent under windy conditions. The wind whips young shoots, tearing leaves from the plant, and rapidly dries plant tissue and soil. Winter wind can be particularly destructive to plants; ideally wind barriers should be constructed on the west and northwest sides of plants for their protection. Prevailing winds are from the south in Kalispell, Miles City, and Glendive but from the west in most other areas of the state.

What Are Your Climatic Characteristics?

Below are the climatic characteristics for twenty-one Montana cities and towns, according to the Western Regional Climate Center. For more specific conditions in your part of the state, visit the center's Web site at www.wrcc.dri.edu.

	Elevation (feet)	Annual precip. (inches)	Apr to Sep precip. (inches)	50% chance last frost by	50% chance first frost by	50% chance length of growing season (days)	Growing season range (days)
Baker	2,930	13.87	10.35	Jun 21	Sep 25	66	25–110
Billings	3,567	14.33	9.55	May 3	Oct 5	151	111–180
Bozeman	4,900	18.26	11.50	May 28	Sep 15	112	61–155
Broadus	3,030	13.49	9.73	May 20	Sep 16	119	83–163
Butte	5,540	12.74	8.80	Jun 13	Sep 7	83	15–165
Glasgow	2,284	11.11	9.07	May 6	Sep 27	138	118–172
Glendive	2,080	13.91	10.70	May 8	Sep 25	137	95–192
Great Falls	3,363	14.67	10.20	May 11	Sep 24	141	107–169
Hamilton	3,575	12.20	5.86	May 23	Sep 19	119	69–173
Havre	2,584	12.73	8.14	May 10	Sep 21	131	83–179
Helena	3,828	11.94	7.79	May 14	Sep 19	128	83–165
Huntley	3,026	13.26	8.80	May 16	Sep 19	125	89–160
Kalispell	2,965	15.18	8.55	May 19	Sep 18	123	80–150
Lewistown	4,940	23.46	16.30	May 26	Sep 18	117	100–146
Libby	3,600	24.66	9.46	Jul 4	Aug 20	49	1–114
Lincoln	5,150	21.14	12.98	Jun 26	Aug 27	59	10–94
Miles City	2,629	13.11	10.29	May 7	Sep 27	147	102–195
Missoula	3,197	13.51	7.3	May 26	Sep 17	115	69–161
Moccasin	4,300	15.37	11.25	May 27	Sep 16	115	58–156
Philipsburg	5,280	15.17	10.04	Jun 26	Aug 26	59	18–115
wood	2,040	13.02	10.38	May 19	Sep 16	119	108–138

Climate

Microclimates and Your Site

Microclimate is far more important to Montana gardeners than hardiness zones. So what can you do on a small scale to improve general conditions in your yard?

Choose the correct exposure. Most flowering plants require full sun for maximum bloom. That means they should receive at least six hours of sun each day. Some plants require or will tolerate partial shade, so fit the plant to your site. A southern exposure is bright, hot, and dry. Plants will do well there in summer only if they receive enough irrigation. You may get away with growing Zone 5 plants in Zone 4 on that exposure. However, this southern aspect is particularly damaging to woody perennials in late winter, when intense temperature changes can cause frost heaving, desiccation, and sunscald. A southern exposure may also cause flower colors to fade in summer, when yellow roses may fade to white. A northern exposure is cold, shady, and damp and not considered prime for most plants. Eastern exposures are cooler and more moist than southern and warmer and drier than northern. They receive the less-intense morning sun and are useful for plants requiring partial shade. Western exposures are similar to and sometimes slightly hotter and drier than southern exposures. The sunlight is intense and winter sunscald, sun scorch, and wind damage are particular problems.

Buildings can block the wind but can make microclimates more complex. For example, plantings on the south side of a house, particularly a light-colored one, are strongly prone to desiccation and winter sunburn.

Most plants within 10 feet of the north side of the house receive too little sun. Their soils remain damp and cool, and you will have trouble with moss in the lawn.

Evaluate your slope. A gentle, nearly flat slope of less than 1 percent grade (a drop of 1 inch in 8 feet) allows cold air to drain away from your planting, thus reducing damage from late spring frosts. Because of this air flow, humidity around the plant canopy is reduced, decreasing the incidence of diseases. A greater slope makes plant maintenance difficult. Never plant in a depression, or pocket, where cold air can stagnate, increasing humidity and the incidence of frost and diseases. Soil in these pockets may be poorly drained and impede root growth of your plants.

Work with, not against, existing vegetation. The shade from trees can interfere with growth of other plants by blocking the  sunlight. Additionally, the roots of most trees extend a distance of one-and-a-half to two times the distance of the dripline from the trunk and will compete for water and nutrients with roots of other plants. Do not plant within the root zone of existing trees unless your plants do well in partial shade and you can supply sufficient water and nutrients for their growth.

Most lawn grasses are aggressive and vie successfully with other plants for water and nutrients. Keep grass away from new plantings of trees and shrubs until they become well established; keep it away from flowers and vegetables forever. Some trees and grasses also compete chemically with other plants by releasing substances from their roots or leaves that prove toxic to some other species. This is called "allelopathy." Some plants are particularly susceptible when planted in the vicinity of black walnut trees or fescue grasses. See http://gardenguide.montana.edu for more details on allelopathic plants.

Use season extenders. If your growing season is too short for that special annual crop, use a season extender—such as a cloche, Hot Kap, or Wall O' Water—to let you set the plants a few weeks earlier than you normally could. Whenever possible start plants from seed in a hot bed, cold frame, or a greenhouse. Montana gardeners can't direct seed tomatoes and expect to get a good crop, but you can succeed planting eight-week-old plants in the garden.

A Montana Time Line

A gardening time line is simple in concept but difficult in application. In Montana especially, local conditions vary so much that it is difficult to predict too far ahead when to plant a species or perform a gardening chore. Following are some general planting guidelines adapted from *A Montana Gardener's Book of Days* (Montana State University Extension Bulletin EB 165; see chapter 12). Fine-tune these to your specific site with more information provided in later chapters.

January. Sharpen hoes and pruning shears; discard damaged stored corms and bulbs.

February. Force rhubarb; force branches of early-flowering shrubs; seed some bedding plants in the greenhouse; cut scions for grafting.

March. Treat thrips-infested gladiolus corms; start crucifers; dig overwintered parsnips and salsify before growth begins; remove winter mulch from perennial beds.

April. Prune fruit trees and bushes; prune ornamentals as needed; remove black knot from chokecherries; apply dormant oil; uncover strawberries; plant peas, onion sets, and asparagus crowns; plant roses; divide perennials like asters and phlox; fertilize perennial beds; remove trunk wraps; transplant most trees and shrubs; roll, seed, and sod lawns; fertilize high-maintenance lawns; start vegetable transplants.

May. Abort crab apple fruit; in early May plant peas, lettuce, spinach, carrots, beets, parsley, Swiss chard, parsnips; in late May plant corn, celery, turnips, and snap beans; harden seedlings for transplanting; start cucurbits indoors; plant sweet peas, morning glories, early gladiolus, and hardy annuals; deadhead spring-flowering bulbs; top-dress peonies; fertilize lawns.

June. Thin fruit; plant tender bulbs, lima beans, peppers, pumpkin, squash, watermelon, eggplant, muskmelon, and tomatoes; prune spring-flowering shrubs; pinch annuals, pine candles, and flower stalks of rhubarb; divide spring-flowering bulbs; transplant container trees and shrubs.

July. Cease harvesting rhubarb and asparagus and fertilizing woody ornamentals early in the month; harvest raspberries, gooseberries, currants, peas, and other garden produce; cage tomatoes; transplant bearded irises and poppies; deadhead roses.

August. Top-dress strawberries after harvest; pinch tops of indeterminate tomatoes early in the month; harvest corn, onions, garlic, and cabbage; sow hollyhock seeds; reduce watering to help plants harden; transplant lilies.

September. Harvest all fruit and vegetables, except root crops; ripen tomatoes in a paper bag; plant garlic mid-September to mid-October; plant spring-flowering bulbs and peonies; seed or sod lawns; fertilize lawns early in month; dig tender bulbs and corms;

fertilize woody ornamentals when leaves drop, if needed; transplant trees and shrubs; apply organic matter and sulfur to the garden if needed; begin fall watering when leaves begin to drop.

October. Apply tree wraps and vole protection; cease planting lawns, trees, shrubs, and perennials by Columbus Day; mulch garlic in eastern Montana; fertilize lawns; discontinue fall watering when the soil freezes; clean and sharpen equipment.

November. Winter mulch strawberries when the soil freezes; prune dead branches.

December. Inspect stored bulbs for damage; keep house plants cool and yourself warm.

CHAPTER THREE

Water Relations

Having sufficient water for plant needs is a supreme challenge for Montana gardeners all year round. Water is scarce in these parts. In this chapter you will find great information on just how water is used by plants and some tips on how to conserve the water you have.

Water 101

We all know that water is essential—but why? Without water a plant's entire physiology shuts down and the plant quickly dies. Water cools and softens the soil, dissolves nutrients for absorption and transport by the plant, and cools the surfaces of the leaves, permitting biochemical reactions to proceed in weather normally too hot (more than 85 to 90 degrees Fahrenheit) for best plant growth. How much water a plant needs depends upon its species and age, the extent of its root system, whether it stands alone in the landscape or is part of a mass planting, whether it is clean-cultivated or mulched, the soil type, the exposure, relative humidity of the air, and the amount of wind at the site.

For example, alfalfa needs 700 tons of water to produce 1 ton of plant material, and wheat needs 500 tons of water to produce 1 ton of grain. But remember, due to runoff and evaporation, perhaps only a third of the water you apply actually gets into the plant, making application of about 2,100 tons of water necessary to produce 1 ton of alfalfa.

Insufficient watering leads to stunted growth, wilt, poor development of flowers and fruit, and premature fruit maturation; excessive watering leads to rotted seeds, restricted root growth, stunting, wilt, and dead plants.

Water infiltrates compacted soils with great difficulty, so watch for several signs and amend the soil as needed. Compacted soils:

- Have dark streaks on the surface.
- Have puddled areas.
- Are difficult to work.
- Result in discolored plants with nutrient deficiencies.
- Impede a plant's vertical root growth.
- Interfere with seed germination.
- Stunt plant growth and reduce yields.

Parts of Montana are experiencing unprecedented housing development at this time, and soils immediately around many new homes have been heavily compacted by construction machinery and ill prepared before landscaping. Be sure to amend the soil *before* you plant; doing so afterward is impossible.

The rule about giving plants at least 1 inch of water per 1,000 square feet per week during the growing season works back east but not in Montana. ("One inch of water" means that if no water drained from a site, you would apply enough water to make a puddle 1 inch deep over a given area.) That rate amounts to about 623 gallons of water over 1,000 square feet of gardens and lawns or over 1,000 square feet of dripline area of trees and shrubs. Applied at the rate of ten gallons per minute (the flow rate found in many outside spigots), it would take a bit over an hour to apply an inch of water.

But that amount is usually insufficient during Montana growing seasons. Instead, estimate the amount of water your plants actually need by looking at pan evaporation. Take a widemouthed container such as a bucket or washtub and make a mark near the top. Fill the pan to the mark with water and place it in an open space at the edge of the garden. Check the water level in a week. If it has dropped 1 inch below the mark, then pan evaporation is about an inch for the week. Since pan evaporation approximates water loss from the plant, you should give your plants 1 inch of water to replenish their supply.

Approximate water needs in inches per 1,000 square feet per week for plants in Bozeman and western Montana are as follows: March 0.50; April 0.75; May 1.5; June 1.75; July 2.5; August 2.75 (early), 1.5 (late); September 0.75; October 0.75 (1 after the leaves have fallen); November, December, January, and February: 1 inch per week whenever the ground is not frozen. Add 0.75 inch per week to all figures for areas in eastern Montana. These are *estimates* of water needs. Do not irrigate if you receive sufficient precipitation for the week. If you can't remember all of those figures, use the following rule of thumb: Give plants about 0.15 inch of water per day in cool weather (maximum temperature 50 to 60 degrees), 0.25 inch of water per day in moderate temperatures (maximum temperature 65 to 80 degrees), and about 0.35 inch of water per day in high temperatures (above 80 degrees).

The bottom line is to ensure the soil in the feeder root zone is kept moist. The feeder root zone on lawns and smaller annuals is about 6 inches deep; on larger annuals, herbaceous perennials, and larger vegetables the feeder root zone is about 8 to 10 inches; and on trees and shrubs, about 12 inches. Deeper watering is even better.

Determining When to Water

Let's take a moment to look at how the soil holds and releases water. Soil texture and porosity influence the movement of water into and through the soil. Ideally, about half of the soil pore space will be filled with water. If more pore space is filled, soil aeration decreases and plant roots suffocate; if less, the soil dries out. The soil is "saturated" when all pore space is filled with water.

The first water to be lost is gravitational water, which easily drains out of the larger pores by the action of gravity alone. When this has happened, the soil is said to be at "field capacity"; that is, it holds as much water as it can against the action of gravity. Because this water is held in very small pores, it is called "capillary water" as opposed to "gravitational water." Capillary water can only be removed by evaporation or by plant uptake. As more water is lost from the soil, the water that remains is held increasingly more tightly and is more difficult for plants to extract. Finally, the point is reached where the water is held so tightly by the soil that the plant can no longer extract it, and the plant has reached the "permanent wilting point." The plant will not recover. The water available between the field capacity and the permanent wilting point is called the "plant available water," or PAW.

There is a point, before the permanent wilting point is reached, when plants wilt under conditions of high water demand, such as in the middle of a hot day when the soil is dry, but recover at night. Plants with large leaves, like squash and cucumbers, particularly exhibit this phenomenon. This is the "incipient wilting point." It is a warning flag of sorts. Soil moisture levels that have been depleted to this point will impact total crop yield, even if water is applied immediately. If water is not applied, soil moisture rapidly reaches the permanent wilting point.

So the trick is to keep soil moisture levels between field capacity and the incipient wilting point by regular irrigation. Keep the soil in the root zone of your plants moist at all time. Don't waste water, but don't skimp on it either. When soil becomes dry enough to induce incipient wilt, root growth stops and may not resume again until as much as two weeks have passed after you have resumed normal irrigation. By that time total growth and yields may have been reduced by as much as a third.

Check your soil every day or two. If it feels hot, it's likely dry. Squeeze the soil into a ball; if it forms a loose ball that easily breaks when you touch it, soil moisture is about right. Dry soil will not form a ball when squeezed; too wet a soil will form a ball that may ooze water when squeezed and that will take moderate pressure to break. Note, however, that particularly sandy soils will not form a ball even when wet, so this test will not work in sandy conditions.

Watering Tips

- Newly seeded areas require frequent, lighter watering to keep the soil surface moist and promote germination. As the plant's roots extend more deeply into the soil, water less frequently but for longer periods of time to allow for good penetration of the soil profile.

- New transplants need frequent watering until their roots can develop a system substantial enough to provide for the water needs of the plant. This may take from a few years for most woody transplants to a decade or so for some species, such as oak.

- The soil around established plants should be at field capacity in late autumn to give the plants the best chance of absorbing all the moisture they can before the soil freezes. Plants must also be watered during the growing season for the reasons mentioned elsewhere in this chapter.

How to Water

Sprinkling does nothing but waste water. Instead, water deeply to moisten the root zone. Water penetrates a sandy soil faster than a clay soil, but it drains faster in sand; water penetrates clay soils more slowly but is retained for longer periods of time. The slow penetration means that too much water applied at once will only

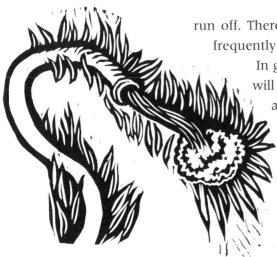

run off. Therefore, water both soils more frequently for shorter periods of time.

In general, in a sandy soil water will have penetrated about a foot after fifteen minutes of watering, about a yard after forty minutes of watering, and about 54 inches after an hour. In clay loams water will have penetrated about 2 feet after four hours of watering.

You can measure the effectiveness of your watering in three ways:

1. Let the hose run for an hour, then dig a small hole about a foot deep to see how far the water has penetrated into the soil.

2. Use tunafish cans placed beneath the sprinklers in several areas of the lawn or garden. When the cans are full of water, you will have applied about an inch and you will be able to judge the consistency of the sprinkling pattern. You can use this method to check the progress on driplines as well. Simply sink the cans into the soil up to their rims and directly beneath the dripline.

3. Take a metal or wooden rod ½ inch in diameter, fit it with a piece of 2x4 for a handle, and push it into the soil. The depth to which the rod penetrates is roughly equal to the depth that water is available to the plant.

All said, watering may require about an hour or two depending upon your water pressure, soil type, and type of sprinkler. The frequency of watering depends upon weather conditions, management practices, species, and soil type, but you may have to water some species three to five times per week. Water in the morning when the temperature is rising; wet foliage at evening is a welcome mat for disease.

Whenever possible water the soil and not the foliage. Plants absorb nearly all of their water through their roots and very little through their leaves. By watering the roots you put the water where it will do the most good, and you eliminate wet foliage, reducing diseases and evaporation and wet fruit, which can crack. Of course it's impossible to not water foliage in a lawn, but you can use soaker hoses in the garden and around trees and shrubs. These hoses are far more efficient in conserving water than sprinklers.

Ways to Conserve Moisture

Montana is a dry state and experiences actual droughts in approximately twenty-year cycles. Even in normal years, with our scant rainfall, water conservation is always on our minds. There are many steps you can take to conserve water.

- Water only when it is needed, and then water well and deeply. If woody plants are growing vigorously, reduce the amount of water you apply by about 15 percent during the next irrigation and watch carefully. At the first signs of wilting, return to your normal watering regime, or apply about 2 inches of water to half the area beneath the tree's dripline and water the other half the following week.

- Some areas of your landscape may need more or less water than others. Adjust your sprinklers accordingly.

- Fix leaky sprinklers.

- Water early in the morning, before the heat of the day evaporates much of the water.

- Avoid use of overhead sprinklers. About a third of the water emitted from these evaporates or is blown off target before it gets to the plant.

- Make sure your soil contains plenty of organic matter to soak up available water and prevent it from draining off.

- Optimize garden crop plant spacing so that the foliage covers nearly all the soil surface. Mass plantings of ornamentals will do the same thing. This shades and cools the soil and reduces water evaporation.
- Raise the mowing height of your lawn in midsummer to about 3 inches.
- Control weeds.
- Use antitranspirants to reduce transpiration of valuable trees.
- Use unsoftened household gray water (water that has been used for washing or rinsing dishes or clothes, not water that should be flushed down a toilet). Treat softened water with gypsum at the rate of a half cup of gypsum per bucket of gray water. Stir, then let the gypsum settle out and use the water for your plants. Even with this treatment, however, long-term use of softened water can cause a sodium buildup in the soil. (See chapter 1.)
- Mulch whenever you can.
- Use drought-resistant plants in the landscape.

Let's look at these last two steps in detail.

Mulch When You Can

Mulches conserve soil moisture, keep the soil cool for root growth, and suppress weeds. They can decrease moisture evaporation by 10 to 50 percent over bare soil and increase the rate of water absorption into the soil. They can warm or cool the soil and can add organic matter or not. Remove all weeds before you apply any mulch.

Mulches can be divided into organic and inorganic groups.

Organic mulches cool the soil and include wood chips, bark, shredded sugar cane, buckwheat hulls, peanut hulls, and ground corncobs. The woodier mulches are best used around larger herbaceous perennials, trees, and shrubs, since they tie up considerable nitrogen during decomposition. Compensate for this by increasing the amount of nitrogen you use to fertilize the plants. Clippings from lawns that have *not* been treated with herbicides are fine for the garden and for annuals. All organic mulches should be applied in a layer 4 to 6 inches deep. They suppress annual weeds fairly well but will do little against perennial weeds and grasses.

- *Straw*: Apply only to warm soil. Use clean straw at rate of one ton per 1,000 square feet of garden.
- *Leaves*: Chop first to prevent matting.
- *Grass clippings*: Okay for gardens. Use day-old clippings from herbicide-free lawns.
- *Compost and rotted manure*: Don't apply fresh manures as mulch.
- *Newspapers*: Shred and soak in water before use; colored print is fine to use.
- *Wood chips, ground corncobs*: Use around trees, shrubs, and perennials only; they require a long time to decompose; high carbon to nitrogen ratio.
- *Bagasse (shredded sugar cane)*: Fibers stick to ripening fruit and to your sweaty back.
- *Peanut hulls, buckwheat hulls*: Expensive; can blow away.

Inorganic mulches (such as landscape fabrics and stones) do not tie up soil nitrogen and are easier to handle than organic mulches, but inorganics are generally unattractive. When used in perennial plantings, landscape fabrics should be covered with a layer of more attractive wood chips. Landscape fabrics and polyethylene mulches are more adapted to use in the vegetable garden, where they can have a profound affect on plant growth. Red polyethylene mulch speeds ripening of tomatoes and peppers and suppresses weed growth, while clear polyethylene warms the soil but does not control weeds. Black polyethylene suppresses weed growth and conserves soil moisture but *does not* warm the soil of the root zone; that is a fallacy propagated by many garden writers. In Montana tests Bob found that the surface of the soil beneath all polyethylene is warmer than the air temperature, but only the soil surface beneath red polyethylene is warmer than the surface of bare soil. At a soil depth of about 2 inches, soil temperature is about the same under all colored polyethylenes.

- *Polyethylene sheets*: Good. Inexpensive. Black does not warm the soil; red speeds early fruit ripening in tomatoes and peppers; clear heats soil but allows weeds to grow.

- *Aluminum foil*: Unsightly. Cools soil less than 10 degrees; increases yields; repels aphids.

- *Stones*: Can be attractive around ornamentals; lay a weed barrier first; can heat nearby plant tissue to cause damage in summer and winter.

Use Drought-Tolerant Plants

All plants require some amount of water, but you can conserve that resource by selecting plants that need less water to thrive. Because of several factors, among them relatively shallow root systems, most vegetables and annual flowers require fairly large amounts of water. Turfgrass is the greatest water guzzler in the landscape. However, many perennials can tolerate prolonged dry conditions and should be considered for planting in your landscape.

It is incorrect to think that drought-tolerant perennials need no water. They need just as much water as any other plant to become established. Once established, however, they make satisfactory growth with less water and tolerate longer dry spells than other plants. Not all drought-tolerant plants are native, nor adapted, to Montana. A list of these appears in the sidebar "Water-Wise Species," but you will find more extensive information in the following chapters of this book. Be advised that you must consider other requirements of the species before you plant. For example, buffalo grass will work better for lawns in hot eastern Montana than for those in cooler parts of the state. Be sure you meet all the requirements for a species before you plant. One size does not fit all plants!

Water-Wise Species

Here is a handy list of selected ornamental species that require relatively little water once established. More plants can be found in the *Tree and Shrub Selection Guide* (MSU Extension Bulletin EB 123 rev.; see chapter 12).

- Amur maple (*Acer ginnala*)
- Box elder (*Acer negundo*)
- Serviceberry (*Amelanchier* spp.)
- Japanese barberry (*Berberis thunbergii*)
- Pea shrub (*Caragana* spp.)
- Silverberry (*Elaeagnus commutata*)
- Green ash (*Fraxinus pennsylvanica*)
- Juniper (*Juniperus* spp.)
- Potentilla (*Pentaphylloides fruticosa*)
- Lewis mock orange (*Philadelphus lewisii*)
- Ponderosa pine (*Pinus ponderosa*)
- Western sand cherry (*Prunus besseyi*)
- Sumac (*Rhus* spp.)
- Black locust (*Robinia pseudoacacia*)
- Rugosa rose (*Rosa rugosa*)
- Russet buffaloberry (*Shepherdia canadensis*)
- Nannyberry viburnum (*Viburnum lentago*)
- Soapwell (*Yucca glauca*)

Grasses
- Fairway crested wheatgrass (*Agropyron cristatum*)
- Blue grama (*Bouteloua gracilis*)
- Buffalograss (*Buchloe dactyloides*)
- Sheep fescue (*Festuca ovina*)
- Hard fescue (*Festuca trachyphylla*)
- Canada bluegrass (*Poa compressa*)
- Russian wildrye (*Psathyrostachys juncea*)

Green Things

Lawns

Lawns are the largest areas of most home landscapes and tie the flower beds, shrubs, trees, and the vegetable garden into a single integrated unit. Lawns dampen noise, cool the yard, and prevent soil from eroding. But lawns can be difficult to maintain attractively in Montana. Poor soil, dry air, and extreme temperatures conspire to make lawn maintenance a full-time summer chore. Having a nice lawn may be difficult, but it's not impossible. We'll show you how to succeed.

Grass Blends

People often ask us to recommend a grass that needs no mowing, no watering, and no fertilizing and that will remain green all year. We recommend artificial turf. If you are willing to deal with the real world, then make an informed selection of the grass that best fits your needs, and go with it.

There are few turf species that do really well in Montana, where winters get too cold for many warm-season grasses and summers too hot and dry for many cool-season grasses. Still, with proper care you can have a respectable lawn. Different species do well in different moisture and temperature regimes and different levels of soil fertility and have different degrees of mowing and wear tolerance, densities, colors, and leaf textures. It is one thing for a species to have all of the great characteristics you want in a lawn, but it is quite another thing for that species to thrive in Montana.

Try to plant a mix of grass species. Each will find its niche in your lawn and blend into a seamless green carpet—maybe. But don't expect your lawn to look like the one on the seed box.

Cool-Season Grasses

Cool-season grasses make up most lawns in the northern half of the United States, including most of Montana. These are the lawns often pictured on the grass seed boxes. If you want a picture-perfect, emerald green lawn, you'll have to work at it in Montana. The cool-season grasses are fairly well adapted to most of Montana, but they will brown out in summer without sufficient irrigation.

Kentucky bluegrass (*Poa pratensis*): Native to Europe. Cold and wear tolerant, this species is the epitome of everyone's lawn grass. It forms a dense sod that rapidly spreads into bare spots. Seeds require up to two weeks to germinate. It is fairly drought and heat tolerant but will brown in just a few days of temperatures of 90 degrees Fahrenheit. Plant in irrigated areas only. Appropriate for western Montana.

Seed Kentucky bluegrass at a rate of two pounds per 1,000 square feet. Fertilize with three to four pounds of actual nitrogen per 1,000 square feet per year. Mow 2 inches high in spring, 2½ inches in summer, and 1½ inches in fall.

Rough bluegrass (*Poa trivialis*): Native to Europe. Slightly lighter in color and coarser than Kentucky bluegrass, this species otherwise resembles the latter. It does well in wet areas and tolerates shade quite nicely but will brown in the summer heat. Because high moisture favors this species, it becomes a patchy weed in heavily irrigated lawns. Use it around the edges of ponds and irrigation ditches where appearance will be secondary to function. Good for use in western Montana.

Seed rough bluegrass at a rate of two pounds per 1,000 square feet. Fertilize with two to three pounds of actual nitrogen per 1,000 square feet per year. Mow 2 inches high.

Canada bluegrass (*Poa compressa*): Native to Europe. The species is not commonly used in lawn seed blends. It is a dull blue green color and presents a coarse, stemmy appearance. It does well in low-fertility soils and in low-maintenance and moderately irrigated sites in both western and eastern Montana. It does not tolerate close mowing or poorly drained soils. Consider this for the backyard in areas that will be mowed and irrigated occasionally.

'Reubens Talon' is a good cultivar of Canada bluegrass for Montana. Seed it at a rate of two pounds per 1,000 square feet. Fertilizer needs are minimal. Mow 2 to 3 inches high.

Perennial ryegrass (*Lolium perenne*): Regardless of its name, this grass dies out in Montana after a few years. Use it in mixtures with Kentucky bluegrass in hot, high-traffic areas such as playgrounds or football fields. It germinates in a week, establishes in a month, and tolerates our cold climate fairly well for a few years. Because it does not spread by rhizomes or stolons, it becomes clumpy if undersown, so don't skimp on seed.

> **Sparse Grass under Trees?**
>
> Where shade has weakened Kentucky bluegrass beneath trees, overseed those areas with perennial ryegrass.

Seed perennial ryegrass at a rate of four to eight pounds per 1,000 square feet. Fertilize with three pounds of actual nitrogen per 1,000 square feet per year. Mow 1½ to 2½ inches high.

Annual (Italian) ryegrass (*Lolium multiflorum*): This is an inexpensive grass seed producing a light green turf that dies after the first season. Its only value is in quickly establishing a grass cover until more permanent grasses take hold. We do not recommend it for seeding alone in Montana lawns.

Fine fescues (*Festuca* spp.): Native to Eurasia. These have fine, wiry blades and are useful for low-maintenance, dry, or shady areas in eastern Montana. They do not tolerate wet areas or those subject to high traffic and high fertility and they produce much thatch. The species in this group include creeping red fescue (*F. rubra*), hard fescue (*F. longifolia*), and sheep fescue (*F. ovina*). The latter is quite clumpy and useful only for low-maintenance areas. Fescue-bluegrass mixtures are available for western Montana.

Seed fine fescues at a rate of three to four pounds per 1,000 square feet. Fertilize with one to two pounds of actual nitrogen per 1,000 square feet per year. Mow 2 to 3 inches high.

Tall fescue (*Festuca arundinacea*): Native to Eurasia. This is a coarse, heat- and drought-tolerant grass that produces a very serviceable coarse-textured lawn in sun or light shade. It has good tolerance for trampling and does well with no mowing.

'Alta' and 'Fawn' are cultivars for Montana. Seed with five to eight pounds per 1,000 square feet. Fertilize with two to three pounds of actual nitrogen per 1,000 square feet per year. Mow 2 to 3 inches high.

Fairway crested wheatgrass (*Agropyron cristatum*): Native to Eurasia. Originally a pasture bunchgrass, this species forms a respectable sod if heavily seeded. If mown tall it tolerates wear and drought and is adapted to eastern Montana and the hot areas of western Montana without irrigation and below 5,000-feet elevation. This is one of the species that does well in areas with less than 15 inches of precipitation. It develops a huge root system and greens quickly in spring with a little water.

Cultivars for Montana include 'Ephraim' and 'Roadcrest'. Seed at a rate of three to four pounds per 1,000 square feet. Fertilize with two pounds of nitrogen per 1,000 square feet annually. Mow 3 inches high.

Western wheatgrass (*Pascopyrum smithii*): Also called bluestem wheatgrass, Smith's bluejoint, and Colorado bluestem, this is a hardy, drought-resistant native that spreads by rhizomes. It is adapted to a wide range of soils and is found mostly in eastern Montana. This grass requires irrigation only during extreme drought and produces a turf of fair quality. When extremely dry the leaves roll to become wirelike.

'Rosana' and 'Rodan' are Montana cultivars. Seed with four to six pounds per 1,000 square feet.

Thickspike wheatgrass (*Elymus lanceolatus*) and **streambank wheatgrass** (*E. lancolatus*): These species have poor turf quality but minimum irrigation requirements. They do well in all soils. Both are moderately salt tolerant and create a coarse, low-maintenance turf.

Eastern Montana cultivars include 'Critana' and 'Bannock' thickspike wheatgrass and 'Sodar' streambank wheatgrass. Seed thickspike with three-and-a-half to six pounds and streambank wheatgrass with three-and-a-half to seven pounds per 1,000 square feet.

Weeping alkaligrass (*Puccinellia distans*): Plant this only on strongly alkali soils where precipitation does not exceed 16 inches per year. Keep it mowed closely or it will become quite stemmy. 'Fult's' is a good cultivar. Seed it at a rate of two to three pounds per 1,000 square feet.

Warm-Season Grasses

This group of grasses grows best in the summer when temperatures soar. They will brown out when temperatures cool and will remain a straw color until temperatures warm again the following summer. Most are well adapted to low-irrigation and low-maintenance areas.

Blue grama (*Bouteloua gracilis*): Montana native. A drought- and cold-tolerant grass of the Great Plains that produces a good lawn in eastern Montana with little or no irrigation once it has become established. It greens slowly in spring.

'Bard River' and 'Alma' are good cultivars. Seed with two to three pounds per 1,000 square feet. Mow 1 to 2 inches high.

Buffalograss (*Buchloe dactyloides*): Montana native. This gray green grass is highly drought and alkali tolerant and should be planted in areas of eastern Montana without irrigation. Like blue grama it greens slowly in spring. It can be mixed with blue grama in the proportion of one part buffalograss to two parts blue grama and seeded at one pound per 1,000 square feet. Buffalograss is very drought and heat tolerant but has a short green season. Water every two weeks to keep it green.

Montana buffalograss cultivars include 'Bismark' and 'Top Gun'. Apply two to three pounds of seed per 1,000 square feet. Fertilize with one to two pounds of nitrogen per 1,000 square feet annually. Mow 1 to 2 inches high.

Nix Zoysia Grass

Zoysia (*Zoysia spp.*) is a subtropical grass not adapted to Montana conditions. It browns with the first frost and remains that way until the following summer.

Selecting the Right Grass for Your Site

Highly variable Montana conditions dictate different lawn grasses for different sets of conditions. Whenever possible, sow a mixture of compatible species to take advantage of the small site variations in your yard.

• For lawns in full sun that are irrigated and fertilized on a regular basis, sow a mix of about 60 percent Kentucky bluegrass, 30 percent creeping red fescue, and 10 percent perennial ryegrass. For lawns in irrigated, shady areas, use a mix of about 30 percent Kentucky bluegrass, 60 percent creeping red fescue, and 10 percent perennial ryegrass.

• For lawns in eastern Montana that receive moderate irrigation and fertilization, try Canada bluegrass, sheep fescue, hard fescue, or a turf-type tall fescue. Sow these thickly as individual species, since the growth habit and texture of each are not complementary.

• In very dry areas where irrigation is limited, plant the wheatgrasses. Do not mow these less than 3 inches.

• If your soil is highly alkaline, plant only alkaligrass.

Lawn Establishment

Grading for drainage. To provide good surface drainage, establish your lawn with a minimum of a 1 percent slope (1 foot drop per 100 linear feet) and a maximum of 10 percent slope away from the house. Grasses not intended to be mowed are very good at stabilizing slopes as great as or greater than 33 percent, provided that the slopes are mulched with straw or covered with cheesecloth to prevent erosion during grass establishment. For slopes greater than about 40 percent, consider terracing at least a portion of the slope and planting it with a low-maintenance ground cover such as creeping juniper to maintain soil stability.

During grading do not add a layer of new soil over existing tree roots! This so-called backfilling around trees and shrubs, even with as little as 1 inch of soil, can slowly kill mature trees by suffocating the roots. Rather, raise the grade around trees and shrubs after constructing tree wells.

Tree wells are used most frequently to spare a tree from damage caused by backfilling to raise the grade of the surrounding area. To create a tree well, a half dozen or so perforated plastic pipes are laid on the original soil surface. The pipes extend from a few inches away from the tree trunk to the dripline and are arranged around the tree like spokes on a wheel. About 2 to 3 feet away from the tree trunk, a wall is constructed that will surround the tree and be at least as high as the final soil grade. This is the "tree well." The perforated pipes run beneath the wall, carrying oxygen to the tree's root system and providing for adequate soil gas exchange. Crushed stone is placed over the pipes out to the dripline to prevent soil from clogging the holes, and then the area is backfilled. The well itself may remain unfilled or be filled with coarse crushed stone to prevent people, pets, and debris from falling into it.

Proper lawn soil. Sandy loam is ideal for lawns. If you need more sand, apply coarse bank sand. Increase your soil organic matter to about 5 percent by adding compost, rotted manure, or peat moss. Soils in much of the state will benefit from tilling a 2-inch layer of organic matter—that's about three or four cubic yards of organic matter per 1,000 square feet—into the top 6 inches of soil. Add approximately one pound of actual nitrogen to each hundred pounds of organic matter to aid decomposition.

Preplanting fertilizers. Add fertilizer and adjust the soil pH based on results of a soil test. It is especially important to incorporate plenty of phosphorus prior to planting.

Seedbed preparation. Bring soil to a very fine granular condition with thorough tilling. Then roll the surface lightly. As you walk across the soil surface, only your sole prints should show. More firm soil may interfere with germination; less firm soil may allow seed to be buried during settling.

After rolling, fill low spots, level high spots, and roll once again to attain an even grade of fine soil. Any unevenness in the grade will detract from the appearance of your future lawn and will be impossible to mitigate later unless you redo and reseed the uneven area.

Seeding. The best time to seed a lawn in Montana is around Labor Day. The grass will thrive in the generally cooler, moister conditions of autumn, and annual weeds will not compete with grass seedlings at that time. You also can establish a lawn in May, but the grass will struggle going into the hot, dry summer, and annual weeds will crowd the young grass.

Using a mechanical seeder, sow half the seed by moving in an east to west direction; apply the other half in a north to south direction. This will give you more even coverage and reduce the numbers of missed areas. Lightly rake the seeded area and roll with a very light roller to improve seed/soil contact and germination. A loosely textured organic mulch such as clean straw or fine compost will hold soil moisture and speed germination of the seed. Hydroseeding incorporates the grass seed into an excelsior-like substance that is blown onto the site and is particularly useful for seeding slopes and areas otherwise difficult to access. Be advised that it takes about a year for a new lawn to look established.

Sod. Sod establishes quickly but is more expensive than seed. It can be installed any time the ground is not frozen and is especially good for establishing lawns on hillsides or on other areas prone to heavy erosion. Purchase an inspected, freshly cut sod that is dense, well-knit, and cut thinly for faster rooting. The maximum thickness of the root system and attached soil should not be greater than 0.75 inch. Prepare the soil as you would for seeding, then lay the sod as quickly as possible after purchase. If this is not possible, hold the sod in a shady area, spread out grass side up, and dampen it periodically to prevent the roots from drying out.

Moisten the seedbed, then lay the sod so that the borders of the strips gently touch adjacent borders. Do not overlap the ends or the edges. Roll the sod after laying is complete and spread some good topsoil in the crevices between strips. Water the entire area well and often, just as you would water a new seedbed. The roots should mesh with the soil in a couple of weeks, at which time you may back off on the watering slightly.

Watering. Water newly seeded or sodded lawns lightly five to six times per day for about three weeks, then twice per day for about three weeks, and finally once per day for the next month. You may have to water every other day in summer for about two hours each time. In early fall, water twice per week, applying a total of about 1½ inches, then give about 1 inch of water per week after the leaves drop from deciduous trees.

Lawn Maintenance

Once your lawn is established, there is still work to be done. Lawns must receive regular fertilization, be mowed at the proper height, and watered. Occasional aeration and dethatching are important to reduce the possibility of disease infestation. You will also want to keep an eye out for weeds. Time consuming? A little. Rewarding? Very!

Fertilizers

Most of our lawn grasses must receive some fertilizer to look good. This is all the more critical if you remove the clippings and the nutrients they contain. For most cool-season grasses under most Montana conditions, apply two to four pounds of actual nitrogen per 1,000 square feet of lawn per year. Do this over two to three applications so that no more than 1½ pounds of available nitrogen per 1,000 square feet are applied at one time.

Timing of application varies around Montana. Fertilizing in very early spring fosters rampant blade growth with little long-term benefit to the plant. Fertilizing within a month of soil freezeup also serves little purpose, for it leaves too little time for the plant to absorb sufficient nutrients. In much of Montana and for moderate-maintenance lawns, apply fertilizer around Memorial Day (after you have mown the lawn twice), Labor Day, and Columbus Day. Fertilize when the grass is dry and preferably just before a rainstorm.

Use a fertilizer containing sulfur to reduce soil pH and make your grass more resistant to certain diseases such as rust and red thread. Inorganic nitrogen sources give better results in spring and late fall when soils are not warm enough to allow breakdown of organic materials. Low-analysis organic fertilizers such as sewage sludge and plant and animal by-products work best when applied in the early fall.

For some years now companies have promoted a special lawn

fertilizer high in potassium for use in fall fertilization. There is some merit to the claim that the high potassium increases winter hardiness in species other than grass but little research suggests that it does the same in lawn grass. So use these specialty high-potassium fertilizers if you wish, but we doubt they will do anything the regular blended fertilizers won't do.

Iron is important for a healthy lawn. Don't spread rusty nails on the lawn—they don't help the grass and are tough on bare feet! Instead, if your lawn shows signs of iron deficiency, apply ferrous ammonium sulfate or ferrous sulfate according to label directions for a quick fix. For a longer-lasting fix, use chelated iron. Also, some lawn fertilizers contain iron in one form or another. Select these and you need to make only one application.

Mowing

Mow anytime the clippings are ½ inch long when you remove only the top third of the grass blade. In early summer and early fall, this may mean mowing twice per week. Frequent mowing reduces stress on the plant and eliminates the need to collect the clippings. As the clippings decompose they will add up to about a pound of nitrogen per 1,000 square foot of lawn. Sharpen mower blades at least a couple of times each season to reduce tearing of the grass blade and the resultant off-white cast it imparts to the lawn.

In western Montana areas, where snow lies on the ground most of the winter, snow mold can become a problem. Lower the mowing height of your grass to about 1½ inches at the last mowing of the autumn. The shorter grass will mat less beneath the snow and reduce the incidence of this disease. Where snow cover is scant in eastern Montana, keep the grass longer going into the winter. The long blades protect the grass crowns from winter desiccation.

Thatch

Thatch is a problem primarily in heavily fertilized, heavily irrigated Kentucky bluegrass/fine fescue lawns. Decomposition is slow in Montana, and old grass stems and rhizomes accumulate. When "thatch" exceeds ½ inch in thickness, it interferes with air, water, and nutrient penetration into the root zone, making the grass weak and highly prone to drought and weed infestation. It is a myth that grass clippings contribute significantly to thatch.

The best time to remove thatch, or "dethatch," is in the spring just before grass has begun to grow. Depending upon where you live in the state, that may be as early as early April or as late as May.

You may hand rake vigorously with a special rake like a Cavex to remove the thatch, but unless you are a masochist, mechanical dethatching mower attachments and power rakes are a better choice. Using a rotary mower blade fitted with spring fingers can be effective as well, so long as the fingers penetrate the thatch layer.

Aeration

Removing plugs of sod where thatch is heavy and/or soil compacted is better than using standard dethatching machines. This is best done on moist soil with core aerator machines that remove cores ¼ to ⅜ inch in diameter and 3 to 4 inches deep. Under extremely poor soil conditions, fill the holes with soil amendments such as sand, peat, or gypsum. Popularly touted devices that use solid spikes to "aerate" the lawn may actually contribute to soil compaction.

Watering

Water as heavily and as infrequently as possible for the soil you have. Frequent, light waterings on soil with good water infiltration and retention properties weaken the finer lawn grasses and promote infestations of weeds such as annual bluegrass and rough bluegrass. On the other hand, overwatering saturates the soil, suffocates the grass roots, and leaches nutrients.

Disease Control

Fortunately, not many diseases attack Montana lawns. Sulfur-containing fertilizers reduce disease incidence because the sulfur acts as a fairly good fungicide. Nevertheless, overfertilization, overwatering, poor thatch control, and improper mowing all can contribute to the following lawn disease problems.

Fairy ring (many mushroom-forming fungi). This is the most common fungus problem attacking Montana lawns. The arcs or semicircles of lush green turfgrass are unsightly and nearly omnipresent. Sometimes two rings will appear, separated by a ring of dead grass. Mushrooms grow at the periphery of the green rings. *Do not* eat these mushrooms unless you can positively identify them as being nonpoisonous.

Fairy rings occur almost anywhere in the state but are most prevalent on light, infertile, dry soils. The fungi that form fairy rings live on the decaying organic matter in the soil, so soil containing old crop residues, heavy thatch, or wooden building scraps can quickly become infested.

There is no practical "fairy-ring getter" for the homeowner on the market. Instead, a combination of heavy watering, aeration, and a regular fertilizer regime will help mask the rings.

Replacing the infested soil with clean soil and reseeding is another way to rid your lawn of fairy rings, but means a lot of work and in most cases is impractical.

Snow mold (*Typhula* and *Fusarium* spp.) grows beneath the snow, especially if the snow has laid in place most of the winter. It appears at the edge of the spring snowmelt as a fuzzy, cottony mass of mycelia, followed by the appearance of greenish yellow patches of dead grass. As these enlarge they may develop a gray color (*Typhula* spp.) or a pink color (*Fusarium* spp.). As the weather warms the patches increase in size and can cause extensive damage to the lawn. Rake out the dead grass as you see it in spring and reseed the area if necessary. To reduce the incidence of snow mold, avoid heavy nitrogen applications in the fall, dethatch regularly, rake leaves from the area, and lower the mower height to about 1½ inches during the last mowing of the autumn.

Melting out (*Drechslera poae* and *D. triseptatum*).Warm, wet springs promote the spread of this disease through lawns of Kentucky bluegrass/fescue. The lower leaves of the grass yellow and the lawn generally thins. Individual leaf blades may have maroon-colored spots surrounded by a yellow zone.

Fertilize moderately (two to three pounds of actual nitrogen per year) and be sure to water properly only in the early morning. Mow the grass as tall as recommended and dethatch on a regular annual basis. Effective fungicides are available.

Powdery mildew (*Erysiphe graminis*).With this disease white dust appears especially on the lower leaves of the grass, which may eventually yellow and pucker. The disease is prevalent mostly during the cool, wet periods of spring and fall, especially in damp, shady areas that are heavily fertilized. Use a blend of shade-tolerant grasses and keep ornamental plants pruned to minimize shade and improve air circulation. During spring and fall, raise the mowing height to the maximum recommended and use only moderate amounts of fertilizer.

Weed Control

A healthy lawn is too competitive for most weeds. If a problem exists, physically remove the weeds or use a recommended herbicide to kill them. Always identify your weed problem, choose the right herbicide, and follow directions on the label. Spray when the air is calm and direct the spray away from desirable plants. Increasing the mowing height will help the grass resist weed invasion and shade germinating weed seeds.

Crabgrass: This is rare in Montana. What most people call crabgrass is any coarse grass in the lawn. Unless that grass is an annual, most "crabgrass killers" will be ineffective.

Quackgrass: There is no quackgrass killer on the market that targets only this species. Careful and repeated application of a systemic herbicide like glyphosate to the quackgrass only will eventually rid your lawn of this weed. Read and follow the label directions carefully.

Broadleaf weeds: Dandelions, thistle, kochia, lamb's-quarter, and pigweed are in this category. Use a general broadleaf weed killer containing 2,4-D or 2,4-D and dicamba and follow directions carefully. This herbicide combination can heavily damage shrubs that it contacts by spray drift or root absorption.

Insects

Our lawns have enough pests, but insects are not one of them. While not insects, earthworms create the most concern for home gardeners. Their castings are unsightly and their burrowing creates mounds in the lawn. But never mind. Don't bother them. They are far more beneficial to the lawn than damaging. They aerate the soil with their burrows and digest organic matter to make nutrients contained therein more available for plant use.

Other Lawn problems

Female dog urine damage is one of our most common problems. The urine, high in ammonia and salts, can leave burned patches in the lawn about 6 inches in diameter. If a female dog frequents one area of the lawn, the entire area will die out. If you observe the dog doing the damage, flush the spot with water immediately. Otherwise the best way to control the damage is to train your dog to go in another area. There are no quick remedies for this sort of damage. If the grass has died, rake out the dead patch and reseed.

At the beginning of this chapter we told you that lawns can be tough to keep nice in Montana. We hope by implementing some of the suggestions in this chapter, the job won't be quite as intimidating.

Vegetables

Growing vegetables in Big Sky Country is challenging. From the high pH soils of eastern Montana to the short seasons in the Rocky Mountains, gardeners always face some adversity. But Montana gardeners are up to the test, gamely trying to grow food for their families but often without good guidance, as most vegetable gardening books do not address Montana's special conditions. We're going to remedy that lack of Montana-specific information in this chapter. You'll find everything you need to grow great vegetables right here.

Plan First, Plant Later

First things first. Growing season matters in Montana. Some vegetables in general and certain varieties in particular take too many days to mature to be planted in every location in the state. To determine your growing season, find the average last frost date in spring and the average first frost date in fall from chapter 2 or from your MSU county extension agent. Count the number of days in between and you have your approximate growing season.

As we discussed earlier in this book, however, some vegetables—especially the warm-season vegetables—stop growing at temperatures well above freezing, so add days to compensate for this. Also, remember that realistically, your vegetables will take

Planting to Market Maturity

The following table lists the average days to maturity of early varieties under optimum growing conditions. Maturity will depend on
season, latitude, production practices, and other factors. The temperature ranges given indicate the optimum soil temperature in
degrees Fahrenheit for seed germination. Under the "relative resistance to frost and light freezes" heading, the word *hardy* means the
plant withstands hard freezes; *half-hardy* means you should plant a
couple of weeks before average date of last frost; *tender* means
plant about a week after average date of last frost; and *very tender*
means plant two to three weeks after the average date of last frost
when the soil has warmed to about 70 degrees. An asterisk indicates days from *transplant*, not from seed starting.

Crop and days to maturity	Cool or warm season	Relative resistance to frost and light freezes
Short-season crops		
Bean, snap: 48 days	Warm (65°–85°)	Tender
Carrot: 50 days	Cool (50°–85°)	Half-hardy
Cauliflower*: 50 days	Cool (50°–85°)	Half-hardy
Chard, Swiss: 50 days	Cool (65°–85°)	Half-hardy
Cucumber, pickling: 48 days	Warm (65°–85°)	Very tender
Eggplant*: 50 days	Warm (65°–85°)	Very tender
Lettuce, leaf: 40 days	Cool (50°–65°)	Half-hardy
Onion, green: 45 days	Cool (65°–85°)	Hardy
Peas: 52 days	Cool (50°–70°)	Hardy
Radish: 22 days	Cool (50°–65°)	Hardy
Spinach: 37 days	Cool (50°–65°)	Hardy
Squash, summer: 40 days	Warm (65°–85°)	Very tender
Long-season crops		
Brussels sprouts*: 90 days	Cool (50°–65°)	Hardy
Corn: 63 days	Warm (65°–85°)	Tender
Muskmelon: 85 days	Warm (65°–85°)	Very tender
Onion, dry : 90 days	Cool (65°–85°)	Hardy
Pepper*: 50 days	Warm (65°–85°)	Tender
Pumpkin: 100 days	Warm (65°–85°)	Very tender
Squash, winter: 85 days	Warm (65°–85°)	Very tender
Tomato*: 50 days	Warm (65°–85°)	Very tender

one to two weeks longer to ripen than the packet says due to our cool night temperatures.

Next, calculate your transplant start dates. Using a calendar, count back from your planting date the number of weeks needed for your plant. Note the date and start your transplants then! If your seed packet does not give information on growing transplants, figure that it will take roughly four weeks to grow a good transplant of a vine crop such as squash and melons, six weeks for crucifers such as broccoli and cabbage, eight weeks for tomatoes, and ten weeks for peppers and eggplants.

Plan your garden carefully in the dead of winter, before the advent of warm weather clouds your reasoning with unrestrained and often irrational excitement! As you plan your garden, keep these pointers in mind:

1. Don't be overenthusiastic. The tendency is to plant a bigger garden than you can care for. It's easy to plant, but who will water, weed, harvest, and "put up" your bounty? Keep the garden a joy, not a chore.

2. Don't plant what you won't eat.

3. Plant a little extra if you can or freeze to reward those Thanksgiving diners.

4. Draw a map. Plan your garden when those seed catalogs arrive at Christmastime. Thinking about the sun on your back and seeds in the soil is very therapeutic during the long, cold Montana winters! Place tall crops on the north side of the garden so they don't shade shorter crops, and put perennials to the side so they don't get in the way of tilling. Place early-season crops together so they may be replaced by later crops (if feasible) or by cover crops to build the soil and reduce weed impact.

5. Choose a level or very gently sloping site. Low spots can be wet and cold in spring. Your site should receive eight to ten hours of sun per day. Avoid planting too close to buildings. If you must plant near a building, plant shade-tolerant crops and increase available light by mulching with aluminum foil.

Putting Up Your Produce—Safely

Montana State University Extension Publications has free, downloadable MontGuides to help you put up your produce. Find them at http://extn.msu.montana.edu/publications.asp. In particular, check out *Freezing Vegetables* (MT198331HR); *Home Canning Pressures and Processing Times* (MT198329HR), which includes elevation charts for Montana county seats; *Canning Pickles and Sauerkraut* (MT199607HR); and *Processing Fruit, Tomatoes, and Mixtures in a Pressure Canner* (MT198803HR).

Dr. Lynn C. Paul, MSU extension food and nutrition specialist, gives us some important canning advice: "Preserving Montana's food bounties may be a family tradition for some, but for others it may be the first attempt. But either way, preserving foods requires an understanding of three key areas.

"The first priority is safety of preserved foods," she states. "You can safely preserve foods by following recommendations that have been tested to ensure you and your family preserve foods that are safe to eat and prevent botulism.

"The second priority is that each person canning food in Montana needs to determine their elevation," Paul continues. "Elevation makes a difference in recommended processing times and pressure. While water boils at 212 degrees Fahrenheit at sea level, it boils at a much lower temperature at higher elevations. Consequently, home-canned foods in Montana *must* be processed with adjustments for our higher elevations. USDA and Montana State University Extension publications all specify times and pressures for specific elevations, *but commercial canning books usually provide information for sea level only.*

"The third key area is understanding that creativity and canning recipes are not a safe combination. Some people think that any recipe or food can be canned at home, but that is not the case. Safe canning recipes require the right mixture of ingredients, equipment, times, and pressure. So play it safe and follow the tested recipes exactly. Never substitute ingredients or guess on processing times and pressures," she warns.

6. Wind reduces yield. If you live in Livingston, Big Timber, or another very windy area, build or grow a windbreak.

7. Trees and shrubs compete with vegetables for light, nutrients, and water. Don't plant close to them, and by all means, stay away from black walnut trees. Black walnuts are allelopathic, meaning they excrete a substance that is toxic to many plants.

8. Rotate your crops. Don't plant related vegetables in the same spot for at least three years.

Nitty-Gritty Down and Dirty

A vegetable garden starts with soil. A deep, well-drained sandy or silt loam soil is best. If you live in eastern Montana (or know someone who does), this is a simplistic statement, as there are few soils in that neck of the woods that would qualify as good loam. Soils that are less than ideal must be amended to increase drainage, reduce compaction, and often lower soil pH.

Commonly used soil amendments for Montana include:

- Acidifying amendments, such as pelletized sulfur, lime sulfur, iron sulfate, and aluminum sulfate. Application rates vary with

Optimum Soil pH Ranges for Vegetables

- Asparagus: 6.0 to 8.0
- Beets, peas, spinach, summer squash, cabbage, muskmelons: 6.0 to 7.5
- Lettuce, onion, radish, chives, cauliflower: 6.0 to 7.0
- Sweet corn, pumpkins, tomatoes: 5.5 to 7.5
- Beans, carrots, cucumbers, peppers, some squash, parsnips, rutabaga: 5.5 to 7.0
- Eggplant, watermelon: 5.5 to 6.5
- Irish potatoes: 5.0 to 6.5

soil type and pH. Follow label directions carefully.

- Organic matter, including compost, animal manures, and plant materials.
- Amendments to improve drainage or reduce compaction, such as coarse sand and organic matter.

Don't wait until spring to apply organic matter to your garden or it won't have time to decompose prior to planting. Fall is the best time to add these materials. If you do put down organic matter in spring, you will need to apply additional nitrogen to facilitate breakdown of the material. Apply compost, manure, and any plant residues from harvest and till in. Leaves from your trees (don't use black walnut) may also be tilled into your garden, but don't apply them too heavily or they will form an impenetrable mat.

Chapter 1, "Soil," tells why fertilization is no simple matter in Montana. The amount you will need to apply depends on the soil in your backyard, not ours! Have your soil tested by a professional lab once every three years and follow the laboratory's recommendations.

Practice crop rotation. Group soil-building crops together one year, follow with heavy feeders the next year, and then grow light feeders the year after. If you have room, include a cover crop in your rotation. Legume cover crops fix nitrogen and build the soil, and nonlegume grasses are considered superior to legumes for weed suppression. Growers may choose to use either legumes or nonlegumes individually or a combination of one of each.

Buckwheat is a fast-growing nonlegume grass (grain) cover crop that suppresses weeds and decomposes rapidly. It is very effective when followed by winter wheat. Barley is good for use in vegetable rotations and does not host vegetable diseases. Oats protect the soil and suppress weeds.

Appropriate legume cover crops include red and white clover and any one of a number of field peas. Austrian winter pea is commonly sold in Montana. Be warned that white clover can reseed itself easily and become a pest!

Use cover crops/smother crops in rotation—inserting a grass-type cover crop in your rotation allows for broadleaf herbicide application. Cover crops suppress weeds, add nutrients, prevent soil erosion, and break insect/disease cycles (see chapter 11). When choosing a cover crop, consider your soil type and climate, seed cost, effectiveness of the crop in suppressing weeds, and the crop's nitrogen-fixing ability. Contact your local MSU County Extension Office or a local seed company for assistance.

To till or not to till—that is the question. Rototilling your garden mixes the upper layers of soil, as opposed to deep plowing, which is no longer recommended. Deep plowing or tilling can cause compaction, buries organic matter too deeply to be of any use, and upsets the microorganism balance. Tilling in organic matter in the fall allows for decomposition and incorporation prior to the next growing season, permits earlier spring planting, and exposes pests and perennial weeds to winter weather, thereby killing them or inactivating them through burial. Fall tillage also exposes heavy soil to alternate freeze-thaw cycles that will help it break down. If you have sandy soils, spring tilling is better, and most gardens need to be tilled again in the spring anyway to smooth the seedbed.

Seed Selection

Perusing seed catalogs at Christmastime is one of life's little pleasures. Deciding between prolific, disease-resistant hybrids or nostalgic, open-pollinated heirloom varieties is part of the fun. In this section we list one or two varieties of each vegetable for you to try, but understand that there are hundreds of choices from which to pick. Seed packets tell you how many days are required for that variety to reach harvestable maturity. Select short-season varieties for a sure crop, and experiment with longer season versions. Ask your neighbors what they have grown successfully. Varieties listed as All-America Selections (AAS) are proven winners under many growing conditions throughout the United States. Vegetables have been bred specifically for productivity, disease resistance, freezing characteristics, and for many other desirable traits. Pay attention to detail and enjoy!

The following vegetable cultivars are good bets in Montana's short growing seasons. The abbreviations indicate resistance to certain insects, diseases, or conditions; see the explanation in the key at right.

Asparagus: 'Jersey Giant' (perennial). F, Cr, R, C.

Bean (bush): 'Provider' (50 days). BMV, DM, PM.

Bean: 'Kentucky Blue' (58 days). AAS Winner; a 'Kentucky Wonder' and 'Blue Lake' cross.

Beets: Any cultivar.

Broccoli: 'Packman' (53 days). Adapted to different climates, including high temperatures, and a wide range of soils.

Cabbage: 'Fast Ball' (45 days). Compact, sweet heads.

Carrot: 'Nelson Hybrid' (57 days). Small core with strong tops for easy harvesting.

Key to the Abbreviations That Indicate Resistance

A—*Alternaria alternata* (crown wilt)
BMV—beet mosaic virus
C—cold
Cr—crown rot
DM—downy mildew
F—*Fusarium* race 1
FF—*Fusarium* race 2
N—nematodes
PM—powdery mildew
R—rust
S—scab
St—*Stemphylium* (gray leaf spot)
T—tobacco mosaic virus
V—*Verticillium*

Cauliflower: 'Amazing' (68 days). Self-blanching, tolerant to cold and heat stress, holds well.

Chard: Any cultivar.

Corn: 'Northern Xtra-Sweet Hybrid' (67 days). An early super-sweet with 9-inch ears.

Cucumber (slicing): 'Diva' (58 days). PM, DM, S. AAS Winner. All-female plants grow fruits without pollination.

Lettuce: Any cultivar of Bibb, leaf, or romaine.

Peas (shelling): 'Wando' (68 days). Heat and cold tolerant.

Peas (edible pods): 'Super Sugar Snap' (62 days). PM. Grows 5 feet tall.

Pepper (sweet): 'Ace' (50 days).
Resistant to blossom drop.
Turns red in 70 days.

Radish: Any cultivar.

Squash (summer):
Any cultivar.

Squash (winter):
'Bonbon
Buttercup' (81
days). AAS win-
ner. A space saver
with small fruits.

Tomato (indeterminate):
'Early Girl' (59 days). Early
and productive.

Tomato (determinate): 'Celebrity' (67 days). V, FF, N, T, A, St. Compact plant

Heirloom Seeds

You cannot save seeds from hybrid crops and expect to get the same variety next year, but you *can* save seeds from heirloom crops. Popular with Montana gardeners, heirloom vegetables have a documented history for at least fifty years and are open-pollinated, meaning the crops are normally self-pollinated or cross-pollinated by other varieties of the same kind of crop. Isolation will maintain the varietal purity and future crops will continue to seed.

The following list indicates the years some heirlooms were introduced and the number of days to harvest. If you grow these vegetables, keep records of your successes and failures.

- 'Lazy Housewife' bean: 1810; 75–80 days
- 'Scarlet Runner' bean: 1633; 65 days
- 'Bull's Blood' beet: 1800s; 35 days for tops, 55 days for roots
- 'Early Jersey Wakefield' cabbage: 1840; 60–75 days
- 'Calabrese' broccoli: 1880s; 58–90 days
- 'Red Russian' kale: 1863; 50–60 days
- 'Oxheart' carrot (Guernade): 1884; 90 days
- 'Country Gentleman' corn: 1890; 88–92 days
- Lemon cucumbers: 1894; 58–70 days
- White eggplant: 1812
- 'Black Seeded Simpson' lettuce: 1850; 50–55 days
- 'Trout Black' or 'Forellenschuss' lettuce: 1792; 55–65 days
- 'Emerald Gem' melon: 1886; 70–90 days
- 'Egyptian Topset' onion: 1700s
- 'Alaska' pea: 1880; 55 days
- 'Nardello' pepper: 1887; 80–90 days
- 'Russet Burbank' potato: 1874
- 'Rouge Vif d'Etampes' pumpkin: early 1800s; 95 days
- 'Fordhook' acorn squash: 1890s; 85 days

- 'New Zealand' spinach: 1770; 50-70 days
- 'Brandywine' tomato: 1880s; 90 days
- 'Riesentraube' tomato: before 1847; 75–80 days

Transplants

Montanans expand the variety of vegetables they grow by extending their season through the use of transplants. Purchase these from your neighborhood nursery or from seed catalogs, or grow your own. Some vegetables take to the transplanting process more easily than others, and some should not be transplanted at all.

Easy to transplant: Beet, broccoli, brussels sprouts, cabbage, cauliflower, chard, lettuce, tomato.

Moderately easy to transplant: Celery, eggplant, onion, pepper.

Special care needed to transplant: Sweet corn, cucumber, muskmelon, summer squash, watermelon. Do not disturb the roots of these during transplanting.

Growing your own transplants from seed is easy. Use a soil-less potting mix to start your seedlings, since garden soil contains microorganisms that may wreak havoc with germinating seeds and young plants. A 50:50 mix of vermiculite or perlite and peat is excellent.

If you have stored seeds from the previous year, test their viability with a "rag doll": Place ten seeds in a paper towel and roll up. Dampen the towel and place it in a plastic bag in a warm spot.

Average Number of Years Seeds May Be Properly Stored

One year: sweet corn, leek, parsnip, onion
Two years: bean, carrot, pea
Four years: beet, pepper, pumpkin, tomato
Five years: brassicas, cucumber, eggplant, lettuce

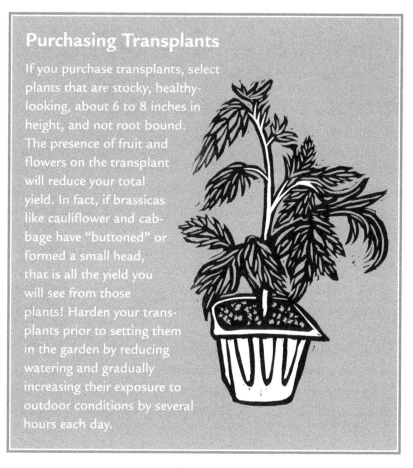

Purchasing Transplants

If you purchase transplants, select plants that are stocky, healthy-looking, about 6 to 8 inches in height, and not root bound. The presence of fruit and flowers on the transplant will reduce your total yield. In fact, if brassicas like cauliflower and cabbage have "buttoned" or formed a small head, that is all the yield you will see from those plants! Harden your transplants prior to setting them in the garden by reducing watering and gradually increasing their exposure to outdoor conditions by several hours each day.

After two weeks, open the doll and count the number of seeds that have germinated; multiply by ten. That is your approximate percent germination.

Start seeds in flats, pots, old cans, margarine tubs, peat pots, and other containers. If you reuse containers, wash with soapy water and rinse with a 10 percent bleach solution. Thin seedlings to one per container for large-seeded plants. Allow herbs to grow in a clump and divide later.

Fill your container about three-fourths full with planting media and insert the seeds at a depth of approximately twice their largest diameter. Water well and cover with plastic to maintain humidity, but don't allow water to stand in the pot.

Give seedlings adequate light. Even a sunny, southern-exposure window will not provide enough light in March and April to keep seedlings from becoming leggy and weak. You can purchase full-spectrum grow lights, but these are fairly expensive. You'll get the same quality of light from a single fluorescent fixture fitted with one warm bulb and one cool bulb.

Water your transplants several hours before transplanting, then set them into the garden in late afternoon or early evening or on a cloudy day. Set plants slightly deeper than they grew in the pot, firm soil about them, and water them well to disperse air pockets.

Your actual date of planting will vary according to your specific conditions. Use the average date of last killing frost in chapter 2 to determine planting dates. Ask your gardening neighbors about ideal dates if you're new to the area. Chances are good that Mr. Pattee next door will be glad to help you!

After transplanting, protect plants from wind and sun for a few days by covering with plastic gallon milk jugs (with cap removed), placing shingles on the windward side, or other means. Keep the soil evenly moist if Mother Nature is being stingy with rain.

"Nurse Plants"

Interplant radishes with carrots. Radishes are quick to emerge and will mark the rows of slow-emerging carrots. Radishes act as a "nurse crop," a crop of secondary importance that will help the primary carrot crop when you pull up the quickly maturing radishes, aerating the soil and thinning the rows.

Direct Sowing

Montana vegetable growers sow much of their seed directly into the garden in rows, in hills, or by broadcasting. To make rows, stretch a string between two stakes or press your hoe handle into the soil to make a straight line. Sow thinly or according to package directions. Mix small seeds with sawdust or coarse sand to help distribute the seeds evenly in the row. Cover with soil and firm it to improve seed contact with soil particles. Water in the seeds to remove air pockets.

Squash, corn, cucumbers, and melons may be planted in hills. "Hills" are not necessarily raised mounds, and in dry areas, hills should *not* be elevated. Hills are simply groups of seeds, usually four to six seeds, spaced 4 to 6 inches apart in each hill. Mound the soil (or not), place the seeds, firm the soil, and later thin the seedlings to three to five plants per hill.

Lettuce, carrots, spinach, and beets are suited for broadcasting in wide rows. Spread seeds evenly, then rake in. Firm the soil and water.

All seedlings, regardless of planting method, should be thinned when necessary.

In good soil, plant seeds at a depth two to three times their largest diameter. If your soil is heavy and easily compacted, cover seeds lightly with soil and cover the row with ¼ inch of sand, compost, or vermiculite to help retain moisture, reduce crusting, and increase ease of seedling emergence.

Picture-Perfect Perennials

When you place perennial vegetables, remember that they are being planted for multiple years, not just one season. Don't harvest from your new perennial vegetables for the first two seasons, and harvest only lightly during the third season.

Rhubarb and asparagus are the most commonly grown perennial vegetables in Montana. Purchase your crowns from reliable local sources. If you order from catalogs, inspect your plants immediately and notify quality control if there is a problem. Watch out for sales! Bargains in the plant world often aren't good deals. Roots should be plump and white, not brown and shriveled or moldy. If you cannot plant immediately, keep the crowns moist by misting or packing them temporarily in damp soil or other media. Keep temperatures constant.

Prepare your perennial bed before planting by digging your hole twice as deeply as needed, then backfill to the right depth. Mix compost into the bottom of the hole. Remember, these plants are going to be in place for years, so do a thorough job. Remove discolored or damaged roots prior to planting. For asparagus, spread the roots of the crowns and place them, bud side up, in a trench 8 to 12 inches deep. Cover the crowns with about an inch of soil. As the stems elongate, continue to cover the tips, 1 inch at a time, until the trench is full. For rhubarb, place the crown so a bud is just visible above the soil level. Firm the soil and water to remove air pockets.

Urban and Intensive Gardening

Do you live in downtown Missoula? Great Falls? Or even Glendive? Don't despair, there's always a way to grow fresh vegetables! You need to plan carefully and use what space you have efficiently.

One of the best urban gardening tools is the raised bed. Two 4-by-10-foot raised beds can produce more than you think. Vining squashes may trundle over the sides and across the lawn. Tomatoes and melons may be trellised. Beans may be poled. If you garden vertically, place tall plants and their supports on the north side of your bed to reduce shading. In raised beds you don't need to follow standard row spacings. You might also consider interplanting, or growing more than one type of vegetable in the same place at the same time. Short-season crops like spinach can be planted among longer-season crops like carrots or beets. (See the sidebar.)

Intensive Plant Spacing for Raised Beds

Plant	Inches apart
Beans, pole	9
Beets	3
Carrots	3
Cucumber	16
Kohlrabi	8
Lettuce, leaf	5
Peas	3
Squash, summer	20
Tomatoes	20

Words about Water

Making a recommendation for watering vegetables in Montana is no simple task. The soils, winds, weather, in fact all of the naturally occurring events we love about Montana make watering less than straightforward.

In general, vegetable crops need 1 to 2 inches of water per week. This water may be applied as irrigation or may occur naturally as rain. One or two good, deep waterings a week is enough for most plants in most soils. After watering, your soil should be wet to 5 to 6 inches deep. For established plants, don't water again until the surface 2 inches of soil is dry. If in doubt, use a soil probe or trowel to check your soil's moisture. See chapter 3 for more details about watering techniques.

The best time of day to water is in the cool of the morning. Watering midday results in high evaporation rates, and watering in the evening encourages disease.

In the soils chapter we talked about the benefits of adding compost or other organic matter to clay and sandy soils. Amazingly, compost increases drainage of clayey soils while increasing the water-holding capacity of sandy soils. Good vegetable gardeners should always try to add organic matter to their plots every year.

Mulches can decrease the need for watering while providing weed control. Mulches can also change the soil temperature, positively affecting some plants while negatively affecting others. See chapter 1 on soils for more information on mulch selection and use.

If you live in Livingston, Big Timber, or another windy location, remember that wind desiccates plants quickly, so more water will be needed. Or you can construct (or grow) a windbreak to reduce water usage.

Soaker hoses and drip tapes are efficient methods of conserving water, plus you don't water the weeds with them! Sprinklers are effective, but up to one-third of the water that is emitted is lost due to evaporation.

Each type of vegetable has a time period when watering is critical (in addition to the seedling stage). Generally speaking, this period occurs during development of the edible portion of the plant. Critical watering periods include:

Mulch-free Rhubarb

Do not apply a heavy organic mulch to rhubarb. Keeping the soil very moist over a long period of time can lead to foot rot, a common problem in Montana rhubarb plantings.

During head development: broccoli, cabbage, cauliflower, lettuce

During root development: carrot, radish, turnip

During flowering or fruiting: cucumber, eggplant, melons, peppers, tomato

Other critical periods apply to other crops:

- Beans and peas: during pod filling
- Corn: during silking, tasseling, and ear development
- Summer squash: during bud development and flowering
- Onions: during bulb enlargement

Weeds

Many weeds infest vegetable gardens, and their control can be time consuming. Whether you prefer the Christmas-control method (hoe hoe hoe!) or the application of herbicides, time is often of the essence.

Purslane, lamb's-quarters, pigweed, quackgrass, and Canada thistle are some major weed pests in Montana vegetable gardens. The best method for their control is to hoe, hoe, and hoe. Besides, it's great for the heart and gives you plenty of fresh air. Keep the hoe sharp and go to it. Be sure to remove succulent purslane as you hoe it, as the plant contains enough moisture to survive on the soil surface long enough to sprout new roots.

For cleaning up large areas, glyphosate is a highly popular herbicide with low residual and toxicity. But don't get any on your vegetable plants as it will kill anything green. Sethoxydim also is registered for perennial grass control in gardens. Always follow label directions when using any herbicide.

Season Extension

Many experienced Montana gardeners routinely extend their growing season. Hot Kaps, Wall O' Waters, cloches, hot beds, and cold frames are frequently used at the beginning of the season to help fend off chilly nighttime temperatures. Row covers are frequently used at the beginning of the season to protect crops as well as at the end of the season to allow time for vegetables to ripen. Many a time gardeners rush out after dinner in autumn to cover their tender plants with baskets, burlap, blankets, or buckets when they hear temperatures will be dropping to 30 degrees that night, hoping that a nice, long, extended warm spell will follow and keep their plants producing.

Greenhousing in Montana requires special research on your part. There are many alternatives from which to select. Heating a greenhouse in wintertime can be cost prohibitive, so you may consider a simply constructed shelter in which to start your seedlings in spring. Consider your application. Do you want a simple structure with a bench in which to start your seeds prior to planting? Do you want a hothouse for summer growing? (It's tough to keep a greenhouse cool enough so plants don't stop growth in summer with our intense sun.) Do you want your structure in place over the garden and yet movable so you may rotate your crops year to year?

"Many of the hobby greenhouses in the marketplace are designed for the milder conditions of the Pacific Northwest," notes David Baumbauer, manager of Montana State University's Plant Growth Center. His advice? "Ask the manufacturer what modifications or accessories are required for the greenhouse to function in your climate. Average minimum low temperature and average wind speed are the two most important factors in determining the heat loss of a greenhouse. High winds frequently damage greenhouses and cold frames with poorly designed fastening systems (poly lock) or ultraviolet-light-damaged plastic film. Pay attention to the quality of the poly lock, and only use greenhouse-grade polyethylene plastic to cover your structure. Other grades of plastic might not have the UV protection additives required to get several years life out of your covering," Baumbauer states.

Special Notes for Special Vegetables in Montana Gardens

Some vegetables are commonly grown in our gardens. The greatest success comes if you know a few tricks of the trade about raising them.

Alliums. Our own university research trials tell us that garlic is best planted in most of Montana between September 15 and October 15. That enables it to establish a good root system before forming leaves in spring. Plant much earlier and the plants are subject to winter damage; plant in November and a great percentage of bulbs will be misshapen. In eastern Montana you have a long enough season to plant your garlic in March. Dig garlic and shallots and pull onions when the tops of three-quarters of the plants have fallen naturally.

Corn. To get the best quality corn, harvest at its peak maturity, and that means sugar! If you're a corn-picking novice, try this: Gently feel an ear. When it feels well filled and the silk has just dried in the last day or so, strip the husk off the tip. With your thumbnail, puncture a few kernels near the middle of the ear. Corn that is ready for harvest will squirt a milky juice onto your thumb.

Nutrient Needs of Some Vegetables

Heavy feeders: Brassicas, corn, potatoes, tomatoes
Light feeders: Cucumbers, lettuce, peppers, squash
Soil builders: Beans, peas, soybeans

At this "milk" stage, your corn contains from 10 to 35 percent sugar. If the juice is clear and watery, the corn is in the "premilk," "water," or even "blister" stage. You'll need to wait a few days before harvest. And if a thick paste oozes from the crushed kernel, your corn has reached the "dough" stage: You waited too long.

Cucurbits. Squashes frequently don't set fruit immediately after flowering. Male and female flowers are almost always found on the same plant, and they rely on honeybees for pollination.

Plants that fail to set fruit may have one of many issues: If there are female flowers but no males, there will be no pollination, and vice versa. Lack of bee activity means no fertilization. The fruits develop slightly, turn yellow, and shrivel. The intense heat of Montana summer days can slow bee activity, as can rain showers and cold mornings near the end of the season. With some varieties, low light (shade) along with high temperatures inhibit female flowers from opening; they shrivel and drop off. With other varieties, low temperatures will cause female flowers to open more quickly than the male flowers.

Don't let your summer squash or cucumbers get larger than about 8 inches long. Larger fruit sends a signal to the plant that its job is complete; that reproduction is assured and there's no need to produce more flowers. There will be no more cocozelle if you allow monster squash to grow!

The old saying about "frost on the pumpkin" really means that the gardener was not good at her avocation. Be sure to harvest all of your winter squash and pumpkins before a hard freeze. With a good leaf canopy, these plants will tolerate a light frost. But once the foliage is gone, any frost will cause chilling damage to the fruit and it will keep but a short time before spoiling.

Legumes. Don't fertilize beans or peas. They will do much better if allowed to fix their own nitrogen. Excess nitrogen will make the plants leafy and lush but won't help production.

Tomatoes. Remove flowers and small fruit from tomato plants around the first of August. It's a waste of the plant's energy for it to try to make more fruit that won't ripen. Removing flowers allows the plant to concentrate on ripening existing fruit. Back off watering your tomatoes and certainly apply no fertilizer after that point. Foliar fertilizers are a bane to many Montana gardeners who use them incorrectly. The idea is to slightly stress the plants. Once your plants have set and sized their fruit, root prune to speed ripening. With a shovel, cut the soil 6 to 12 inches away from the plant in several spots to a depth of about 6 to 8 inches, partly encircling the plant. Don't remove the soil, just slice it. In many instances, you will see those green tomatoes start to color within a few days!

Cold-tolerant vegetables. Brassicas and fall spinach can withstand some cold, and their fine flavor may be heightened after a frost. Kale, carrots, and parsnips can overwinter in some areas of Montana. Be sure to mulch them with 6 to 8 inches of straw if you live where snow cover is sparse.

Perennials. Fall, around early October, is a good time to fertilize asparagus and rhubarb with manure or compost. Do not apply too thick a layer of compost to rhubarb, as that may encourage foot rot. Be sure to cut back dead stalks after the killing frost.

Fruit

Montana is not prime fruit-growing country, but you can harvest some delicious fruit if you choose the right species and pay attention to detail. When experts say that you "cannot grow" this or that fruit in your area, they don't necessarily mean that the plants won't survive but rather that you generally cannot harvest a good quantity of high-quality fruit consistently.

In this chapter we'll talk about strategies for growing both "tree fruit" and "small fruit." Strawberries, blackberries, serviceberries, raspberries, grapes, currants, gooseberries, blueberries, and the bush cherries are what are known as small fruit, sometimes also called "bush fruit." The rest are considered tree fruit.

The Right Fruit for Your Zone

In general, plums, apples, chokecherries, minor stone fruit like bush cherries, serviceberries, currants, gooseberries, strawberries, red raspberries, and buffaloberries will work in Zone 3. In Zone 4 add very hardy grapes, pears, and sour cherries to the list. In the warmer sections of Zone 5, add American- and French-hybrid grapes, sweet cherries, peaches, and apricots, though the latter three may be damaged often by winter cold and late frosts. Many of the small fruit, particularly those with thin canes like raspberries and grapes, will suffer from severe winter desiccation, so you will have to take measures to reduce that.

These zone recommendations are based more on growing season and sensitivity to frost than on plant hardiness. While a species may tolerate low winter temperatures in Zone 3, you may not have a long enough growing season to ripen the fruit. For example, Concord grapes will survive winters in Zone 4 if they are planted on protected sites, but the season often is not sufficiently long for them to fully ripen their crops. Late spring frost can damage the flowers on all fruit, especially on the early-blooming species. While the apricot plant is hardy enough to withstand Zone 4 winter conditions, late frosts destroy the blossoms on this early-flowering plant in most years; it's for that reason primarily, not its lack of hardiness, that apricots are not recommended for general planting in the state. Early fall frosts damage ripening fruit and are particularly problematic on grapes, which ripen later than many species. Fall-bearing raspberries and strawberries may not have a long enough season to produce a fall crop since, in Montana, their first, or "June," crop often does not ripen until mid-July.

For these reasons, note the number of days from bloom to harvest in the sections under the individual fruit and select your varieties accordingly.

How long it takes a fruit plant to set its first crop depends upon the species, variety, stock, and site. Generally, small fruit like strawberries and raspberries will produce the second year and the larger species, like currants and gooseberries, will produce full crops beginning in their fourth or fifth year. Standard apples may require five to twelve years to produce their first crop; dwarf apples, two to three years. Peaches, plums, and apricots need about four years, and the cherries two to three years. Don't get discouraged—it's worth the wait.

Sun and Soil Essentials

Plant all fruit in full sun for the best crops. Be sure you have well-drained soil. No fruit plant does well in poorly drained soils.

As with other aspects of Montana gardening, close attention to detail is crucial. Following are the details we consider very important. Understand them, pay attention to them, and you'll be the envy of your neighbors.

Soil pH: Most fruit species tolerate our alkaline soils, though some, like apple and raspberry, may show signs of iron deficiency when the soil pH exceeds about 7.5. Blueberries, cranberries, and lingonberries—being ericaceous, or acid-loving, plants—do best at a soil pH around 5 and therefore are not recommended for general planting anywhere in the state. Soils in small plots may be specially prepared to accommodate ericaceous plants, but take care that your inputs do not exceed the crop's output. In other words, make sure the endeavor is worth the frustration and the extra effort for a few pints of fruit.

Pollination: Good pollination is necessary for good fruit production. Most fruits are pollinated by insects, notably bees; mulberries and the nuts are wind pollinated; strawberries and Italian prunes are pollinated by both wind and bees. Take care that you have sufficient bees to accomplish pollination and never apply an insecticide to your plants when bees are active.

Many gardeners are confused over the necessity of planting more than one variety of fruit. In general, *all small fruit* are self-fruitful and will set a good fruit crop by their own pollen, so you need only a single variety. However, you will get more fruit if you provide for cross-pollination by planting at least two varieties of the same fruit. Although apricots and sour cherries are self-fruitful, *most other tree fruit* are self-unfruitful: They will set some fruit by their own pollen but the quantity will be inadequate. Therefore, always plant at least two varieties of the same tree fruit or small fruit within 40 feet of each other. Generally, red strains of apples are not reliable pollinizers for their parent strain. For example, don't rely on 'Red McIntosh' to pollinize 'McIntosh', and vice versa.

Diseases: With its dry climate Montana does not experience as many fruit diseases as other states. However, bacterial fireblight is especially destructive on apples and pears. It is imperative that you select resistant varieties of these fruit and take care not to over-stimulate vegetative growth with excess nitrogen and excess pruning; the new growth is particularly susceptible to this disease.

Avoid planting on heavy, wet soils, which can increase the incidence of root and crown diseases in raspberries, strawberries, and grapes.

Sunscald is damage to the tissue beneath the bark caused by intense sunshine and/or sunlight reflected onto the bark from snow cover in late winter. Sunscald most often occurs on the south or west side of the trunks of dark-barked trees like apple and cherry or on trees less than six or eight years old. While not a true disease, sunscald can cause significant damage to unprotected trunks of apple and the stone fruit. Often this damage leads to canker infection and the subsequent demise of the plant.

Failure to Fruit

Failure of a fruit plant to produce a crop can be due to lack of plant maturity, rodent damage to the trunk and roots, low soil fertility and moisture, excessive nitrogen, excessive shade, frost during bloom, drought the previous summer during bud formation, severe winter conditions, chinooks, and an excessively large crop the previous year.

Insect pests: As with diseases, not many insects attack fruit in Montana. Codling moth and maggot on apple, a few other worms on the other fruit, aphids on all fruit, and spittlebug on strawberries will be most of your worries. Apple maggot and codling moth may be a bit difficult to control. You can handpick the fruit worms, spray the aphids with a strong stream of cold water, and pretty much ignore the spittlebugs in most cases.

Other pests: Drape fruit trees with netting to control bird predations, but protection from bears is another problem. These animals are far more destructive than birds, as they often climb into trees and break branches to get at the fruit. An electric fence will work sometimes, but otherwise there is not much you can do for protection here but to avoid planting fall-ripening fruit of any kind where bears are active.

Purchasing and Planting Fruits

From a reliable nursery purchase one-year-old whips or two-year-old well-branched fruit trees 5 to 6 feet tall and of ½-inch caliper, or one- or two-year-old small fruit plants. All plants should be certified true to name and certified disease free, with the variety and, where appropriate, the stock and the interstock noted on the label. Bare-root, balled and burlapped, and container plants are all acceptable. Do not purchase plants that appear stunted or poorly shaped, and do not plant bare-root plants unless they are dormant.

Plant in the early spring before the buds begin to swell or plant in the early autumn. Labor Day is a good time, but use only container and, less preferably, balled and burlapped plants at this time. Do not plant after Columbus Day, as plants may have insufficient time to develop a good root system before winter. Plant currants and gooseberries in the autumn because they begin growth so early in spring.

Fertilizing

All tree fruits receive the same general care. Apply about a quarter pound of a 10 percent nitrogen fertilizer per tree in June of the planting year if trees were planted in spring. Increase this amount each year until your mature trees (six to eight years old) receive about four pounds of a 10 percent nitrogen fertilizer per year. If you planted in the fall, apply a quarter pound of a 10 percent nitrogen fertilizer per tree early the following spring. Fertilize each year in very early spring or in fall after the leaves drop, but do not overfertilize, especially on apples and pears that are prone to fireblight.

For small fruit, apply about two to three pounds of a 10 percent nitrogen fertilizer per 100 feet of row (strawberries and brambles) in early spring (brambles) or after harvest (strawberries). Give grapes, currants, and gooseberries a handful of complete fertilizer per plant in early spring. The nutritional needs of the other small fruit have been studied insufficiently, but giving them a handful or two of complete fertilizer early each spring, depending upon plant size, won't hurt.

Tree Fruit

A home orchard is romantic and certainly a wonderful place to be during spring bloom and fall harvest, but you are a homeowner, not an orchardist. Your space and time are highly invested, so select your tree fruit carefully. A few fruit trees are all most of us can handle.

Pruning Techniques

Fruit trees will grow perfectly well without pruning, but they will not bear large, attractive fruit without careful annual pruning to promote good air circulation and sunlight penetration through the tree.

Prune tree fruit in early spring. Avoid making large cuts that lead to the growth of multiple watersprouts and adventitious shoots, which must be removed. An adventitious shoot is one that arises near a cut surface from a bud newly formed as a result of the injury. This soft, succulent growth on apple and pear is highly susceptible to fireblight infection and, if pruning is done in fall, to winter damage. Your best plan is to prune all tree fruit to the modified central leader system. Here are the steps.

First year: At planting, head back the top of a whip to about 30 inches to force lateral branching. When 2 or 3 inches of new growth have occurred after planting, select up to a half-dozen shoots to become the main scaffold branches. These should be at least 18 inches from the soil surface and spaced around the tree at least 6 to 8 inches apart vertically. If you don't have enough the first year, select what you can and follow up with the second year's growth. Spread these branches to an angle of about 50 degrees, but no more than 60 degrees, from the main trunk with spring-loaded clothespins. This will force the branches to develop wide, strong crotch angles. Allow the most vigorous, most centrally growing upright shoot to remain as the tree's leader.

Second year: Continue selecting scaffold branches until you have a maximum of six to eight main branches. Spread young shoots with a clothespin and somewhat older shoots with a lath notched at both ends if needed to achieve the right crotch angle. Leave these spreaders in place for no more than two years. Pruning will consist entirely of removing unwanted growth that crowds the shoots you have selected as main scaffolds. Continue to allow the leader to grow upward, and continue to select new scaffolds as needed.

Subsequent years: When the tree has reached the appropriate height for its variety and rootstock, cut the leader back to a side shoot. This is "modifying" the leader. Each year prune the tree in early spring, removing suckers, watersprouts, and other unwanted growth, as well as continually pruning the leader to a side shoot to maintain the desired tree height.

Tree Fruit Varieties

There are tens of thousands of tree fruit varieties available, but only a few of the hardiest, most short seasoned, and blight resistant will make it in Montana.

Apples (*Malus domestica*): Apples will produce a reasonable crop in most parts of the state. Trees grafted to M7, EMLA 7, or MM 106 rootstocks produce productive, semidwarf plants about 12 feet tall at maturity. In Zone 3 and on particularly cold sites, choose trees on 'Antonovka' or 'Robusta' #5 stocks for their particular cold hardiness. In these areas interstocks of 'Anoka', 'Antonovka', and 'Hibernal' will lend additional cold hardiness to double-worked trees. Regardless of stock, the varieties you select should be able to ripen their crop in your growing season and should be resistant to fireblight.

For example, in Zones 3 and 4 select summer- and early-fall-ripening varieties. These generally require less than 120 days to ripen their fruit. In Zone 5 all of the earlier-ripening varieties plus some later-ripening varieties like 'Haralson' and 'McIntosh', which ripen in about 145 days, are appropriate.

Apples are ripe when their green undercolor has turned to a yellow green, when their seeds have turned dark brown or black, and when they detach easily from the spur.

Apple Advice

- A spur-type apple tree produces far more spurs upon which fruit are born than a tree with a standard-bearing habit. Many, but not all, varieties have spur-type strains. Purchase these if you can.

- Early-ripening 'Lodi' apples work well at high elevations, ripening in late August at around 5,000 feet and early September at 7,000 feet. Do not plant apples above 8,000 feet. Unfortunately, 'Lodi' is susceptible to fireblight.

These are some varieties recommended for Montana, including their time frame for ripening and their resistance to fireblight.

- 'Anoka': Late summer; unknown resistance
- 'Caravel': Summer; very resistant
- 'Crimson Beauty': Summer; resist
- 'Duchess of Oldenburg' ('Duchess'
- 'Haralson': Late fall; very resistant
- 'Hibernal': Late fall; very resistant
- 'Mandan': Fall; resistant
- 'Puritan': Summer; resistant
- 'Red Astrachan': Fall; resistant
- 'Red McIntosh': Fall; resistant
- 'Viking': Summer; resistant

Pears (*Pyrus communis*): Pears are as hardy as apples, but because of their extreme susceptibility to fireblight, they are not commonly planted in Montana. Consider all pear varieties as self-unfruitful so plant at least two. 'Bartlett' and 'Seckel' are cross-incompatible, and 'Magness' and 'Waite' are pollen sterile. Asian pears are not adapted to Montana.

Pears allowed to ripen fully on the tree often break down at their core. You will have better pears if you pick the fruit just as the undercolor begins to turn to a light yellow green and store them at about 45 degrees for a week or so before you wish to use them. At that time, remove the fruit from storage and place

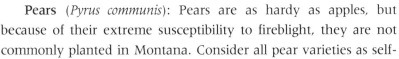

Perfect Pears

- Pears have a strong vertical growth habit. Use branch spreaders liberally to widen the crotch angles.
- Bees are not highly attracted to pear nectar and much prefer to visit dandelion flowers. Saturate your pear planting with bees and control the dandelions for a good pear crop.

them in a room at about 60 degrees. They will ripen just fine at that temperature.

The following varieties will work in areas of the state with sufficiently long seasons. The list is organized by length of season; note the bloom-to-harvest days for each variety.

- 'Bartlett': 110 to 115 days
- 'Gorham': 122 to 130 days
- 'Seckel': 130 to 135 days
- 'Anjou': 135 to 140 days
- 'Bosc': 140 to 145 days

Peach (*Prunus persica*), **nectarine** (*P. persica*), and **apricot** (*P. armeniaca*): These stone tree fruit are not well adapted to Montana. Apricots (both tree and bush types) especially are highly susceptible to late spring frosts, and *if* you can grow them at all, you might expect a crop once in five to seven years. Nevertheless, you may grow the fruit successfully for several years in well-protected sites in Zone 5 until a particularly cold winter takes them out.

As with apples and pears, do not overstimulate stem and leaf growth with excess nitrogen and excess pruning, and you must protect the trunks from sunscald. Lastly, vertical shakes, frost cracking, or trunk split—the problem is known by all three names—is a particular difficulty with stone fruit in Montana due to our fluctuating winter temperatures and the weak nature of the wood. On very cold mornings in the vicinity of minus 20 to minus 30 degrees, the temperature differential between one side of the tree trunk and the other, or between the wood on the inner and outer trunk, causes the trunk to split, often with a resounding pop. Sunscald protection does help a bit, but there is not much more you can do to protect the tree against this type of damage. If you are up for a challenge, try 'Reliance' or 'Redhaven' peaches, 'Harko' and 'Hardired' nectarines, and 'Harcot', 'Veecot', and 'Harlayne' apricots, but don't get your hopes up.

Cherries: Sour cherries (*Prunus cerasus*) are self-fruitful and hardier than sweet cherries (*P. avium*) and will tolerate Zone 4 winters. Purchase the genetically compact 'Meteor' or 'North Star' varieties for easy maintenance. As with the other stone fruit, protect cherries from sunscald and trunk split. Birds and bears are particular problems.

Standard sweet cherries (Zone 5) are for the most part self-unfruitful, and there are a lot of cross-incompatibilities. Therefore, they must be cross-pollinated by the right variety. Some combinations that work are 'Bing' and 'Black Tartarian', 'Napoleon' and 'Van', and 'Lambert' and 'Windsor'. Fortunately for the homeowner there are self-fruitful compact sweet cherries named 'Stella', 'Lapins', and 'Sunburst'. As with the other stone fruit, protect these from sunscald.

Plums (*Prunus* spp.): Several species are suitable for Montana gardens. The European plum (*P. domestica*) works in Zones 4 and 5. 'Stanley' and 'Yellow Egg' are self-fruitful varieties, while 'Italian Prune' and 'Reine Claude' need cross-pollination. The Japanese plums (*P. salicina*) are self-unfruitful and bloom very early in spring; hence they are prone to late frost damage. If these will work anywhere in the state, it would be near Flathead Lake and possibly in the Missoula and Billings areas. The American plums (*P. nigra* and *P. americana*) are hardy and, while not as large or as well-known as other plums, will grow in most of the state, although both species are self-unfruitful. Try 'DeSota', 'Hawkeye', 'Wyant', and 'Wolfe' (*P. americana*) or 'Cheney' (*P. nigra*). American plums sucker badly, so keep the suckers under control with judicious pruning. Finally, hybrids of *P. salicina* x American species are good bets for most of the state. 'Red Wing',

'Underwood', 'Tonka', 'Fiebing', 'Monitor', and 'Pipestone' (the last quite popular in the state) are worth planting. Use a native plum, either *P. americana* or *P. nigra,* for pollination.

Sunscald and trunk splitting are common on plums, as is true of other stone fruit. Also, plums are quite prone to preharvest fruit drop here. Fruits that fail to size properly and fall off in August are most often due to insufficient watering and high temperatures, but heavy fruit set can contribute to preharvest drop as well.

Harvest plums when they are soft and fully colored and detach easily from the tree.

Minor stone fruit: Several less widely grown stone fruit species have sufficient hardiness for planting in Montana. The chokecherry (*Prunus virginiana*) forms a heavily suckering tree which, if left unpruned, becomes a thicket. It is used both for shelterbelts and fruit production in Montana. Winter hardy and prolific, it is adapted to all parts of the state, even into the high mountains at Zone 2. There are purple-, black-, red-, and yellow-fruited forms of this species; 'Mission Red', 'Schubert', and 'Canada Red' are well-adapted varieties. Siberian bush apricot (*P. armeniaca* var. *siberica*) is hardy to Zone 5 but bears very small fruit. *P. besseyi*, the western sand cherry, also a bush, is hardy to Zone 3 and produces small, purplish black fruit. The plant is shallow rooted and suckers badly. The 'Nanking' cherry, or Hansen's bush cherry (*P. tomentosa*), tolerates Zone 3 conditions and produces fruit useful for pies and jams. The plant is adapted to lighter soils but is not as productive as other species.

Nuts: Nut trees are rare in Montana, but the black walnut (*Juglans nigra*) will tolerate conditions in Zone 5 and the warmer parts of Zone 4, though it does not thrive in most areas. It requires a deep, fertile soil and adequate moisture. At best it is very slow growing in Montana. Be warned that the tree produces a compound that is toxic to many plant species, including tomato, potato, blackberry, and apple. Keep these plants well away from the root zone of the black walnut. Additionally, some people are allergic to the walnut pollen and horses may be poisoned by the sawdust and woodchips used for bedding. Plant this tree with caution.

J. cinerea, the white walnut or butternut, is hardier than the black walnut and will tolerate slightly less well-drained conditions.

Late frosts can damage walnut flowers, and rainy weather during bloom may interfere with proper wind dispersal of the pollen. Our short, cool summers, droughts, and strong winds can also cause shriveled or unfilled kernels.

Small Fruit

Plantings of small fruit, also called bush fruit, give you a faster return on investment and are easier to fit into the average landscape than are tree fruit.

Pruning and Training Techniques

Some of the minor *Prunus* spp. and the currants and gooseberries form bushes and hence can be pruned like any other bush. In early spring, before bud swell, remove all damaged or diseased wood and all canes older than about three or four years. Thin out remaining canes so that only about six to eight remain per bush, and thin these to stand about 6 inches apart.

Grapes can be pruned and trained to the four-cane Kniffen system, perhaps the easiest system to master for this crop. At planting construct a two-wire trellis with the first wire about 2 feet off the ground and the second wire about 3 feet above that. Space the trellis posts 8 feet apart. After planting train the vigorous, central shoot up to the first wire on the trellis and continue this in the second year until it reaches the second wire. Select two shoots on each side of this "trunk" that emerge close to the wires and train them to run along the wires. Remove all others so that the vine has just four canes remaining. Fruit will be born on shoots emerging along these canes. In the March after harvest, cut each of the old canes back to a vigorous cane that emerged from the main cane near the trunk and near the wire. Train this cane along the wire to produce the succeeding crop. Repeat the process each year.

Strawberries are not pruned but trained. The most common training systems for the home gardener are the hill system, in which all runners are removed and only the mother plant allowed to remain in production; the matted row system, in which all runners are allowed to set daughter plants wherever they wish; and the spaced row system, in which typically four runners are allowed to remain with the mother plant. These are set at the four points of the compass from the mother and allowed to produce daughter plants. All other runners and daughter plants are removed. The hill system provides the largest fruit but the smallest number of them; the matted row produces the greatest number of fruit, but they are quite small. The spaced row system provides the best of both worlds.

> ## Strawberry Secrets
>
> • Unless you keep your strawberry bed clean and thinned, the planting will run out in a very few years. Renovate an old bed or plant a new bed every three to four years.
>
> • How many strawberry plants should you grow? About twenty-five plants per family member is about right for most Montanans.

Raspberries come in June-bearing and fall-bearing types. The red and yellow raspberries are the most common in the state. In March remove the dead, damaged, and fruited canes of the June-bearing type and thin out the remaining canes to stand about 6 inches apart in the row. With the fall-bearing type, remove the upper 8 to 10 inches of the cane that has fall fruited right after harvest. Thin the remaining canes in March to stand about 6 inches apart, then remove the old canes after harvest in July.

Small Fruit Varieties

Currants and gooseberries: These are very hardy up to around 9,000 feet and will do well throughout the state. 'Red Lake' and 'Perfection' are two great red currants to try. They do not tolerate heat well and so should always be planted on an east exposure and mulched with an organic mulch like wood chips.

Gooseberry fruits are subject to sunburn, so use good management practices to maintain a healthy leaf canopy on the plant to shade the fruit. They also tend to tip layer themselves, meaning the new shoot will bend to the ground and root, forming a new plant. If ten shoots do this, you will have the mother (original) plant and ten daughter plants. So take care to rogue out any layered plant at pruning time. Try 'Pixwell' and 'Poorman' for a delicious crop of gooseberries.

Harvest currants when fully colored by snipping the entire cluster from the bush. Shuck the fruit just before use. Harvest gooseberries when they have attained the full color of the variety.

Grapes: Some species are marginally adapted to Montana; other species suffer winterkill if they see a map of the state. Forget the *Vitis vinifera*, or European grape, which is wholly unsuited to Montana. The hardiest of the French hybrids may work in some of the most protected sites in the warmest areas of Zone 5, but they would be unreliably productive. The American bunch grapes (*V. labrusca*) like 'Concord' are hardy enough to tolerate our Zone 4 winter cold but on many sites will prove unsuitable since our seasons are generally not long enough for the fruit to ripen. Most varieties of American grapes need at least 140 days to ripen properly.

You stand the best chance of ripening grapes, even in warmer areas of Zone 3, that are hybrids of the *V. labrusca* and one of our hardiest natives like the *V. riparia*, or riverbank grape, which is native to Montana. Varieties like 'Valiant', 'Swenson Red', and 'Beta' may work for you. However, grapes that may survive the winter cold may not survive winter desiccation. Provide a snow fence and give them added winter protection by wrapping the vines in burlap or by bending the plant to the ground when it becomes completely dormant and lightly covering it with soil. Unfortunately, the buried canes may look like a smorgasbord to voles.

Strawberries (*Fragaria* x *ananassa*): These will produce a bountiful crop for Montana gardeners, although June-bearing varieties like 'Sparkle', 'Surecrop', and 'Earlidawn' may ripen their fruit in July. Fruit of the fall-bearing varieties like 'Fort Laramie' and 'Ozark Beauty' often are considered to have flavor inferior to the June-bearing varieties, and your season may be too short to ripen the fall crop successfully. A third type of strawberry, the day-neutral, produces berries from spring until fall. This type has been around for only a couple of decades, so its culture has not been thoroughly investigated. It does well in some parts of Montana, however, so long as you give the plants high fertility and plenty of moisture to keep them going. They are high-maintenance plants but may perform very well for you. Try 'Tristar' and 'Tribute' as an experiment, and let us know how you make out.

If you expect little snow cover, apply at least a 2-inch layer of winter mulch after the ground has frozen to protect the plants from heaving. This will be about mid-November. Remove the mulch when growth begins in spring and leave it in the walkways as a summer mulch. (The purpose of a winter mulch is to keep the ground frozen, not to keep the plants warm.) Clean barley straw makes an excellent strawberry mulch. Fertilize the crop only after harvest, since fertilizing in early spring tends to produce excessive top growth and leads to heavy fruit rot activity.

Harvest strawberries by detaching the stem from the plant,

leaving it attached to the fruit. Just before use, shuck the fruit by detaching the cap.

Raspberries (*Rubus* spp.): There are eight types of raspberries —four colors that come with either June-bearing or fall-bearing habits. The most common of these are the June-bearing red, black, and purple raspberries and the fall-bearing red and yellow raspberries. Montanans prefer the red raspberries of both types to all others. These are hardier than the purple raspberries, which in turn are hardier than the black raspberries. The yellow are as hardy as the red but are not popular here. If you feel daring, try 'Fall Gold' yellow raspberry for a real treat. June-bearing red raspberry varieties include the old 'Latham' and 'Madawaska' and the newer 'Boyne'. Fall-bearing varieties suitable for Montana include 'Heritage' and 'Fall Red'.

While the red raspberries are hardy enough for all but the very coldest parts of Zone 3, their thin canes are highly susceptible to winter desiccation. Red raspberry canes lose winter hardiness from the top down, beginning with the first warm days of late January. This, along with wind desiccation, makes the tops of the canes highly susceptible to winter damage. Provide a windbreak to shelter the plants as well as some shade protection on the south side of the planting to reduce damage from winter sun. Sites with heavy, wet soils and poor drainage may be unsuitable for raspberry plantings because of the higher incidence of root and crown diseases.

Harvest raspberries when they are fully colored, soft, and detach easily from their receptacle. Yellow raspberries are ripe when they turn an amber color.

Blackberries (*Rubus* spp.): 'Darrow' erect blackberry is marginally adapted to the Zone 5 areas of the state and may produce a few fruit each year on the best of sites after a mild winter. The thornless evergreen blackberries are not adapted to Montana.

Serviceberries (*Amelanchier canadensis* and *A. alnifolia*) and **buffaloberries** (*Shepherdia* spp.) are adapted to Montana, the latter doing especially well in the eastern part of the state. Both require well-drained sites and little care and both are pruned to bush form following the outline for currants and gooseberries above. A few plants of each should supply the average family with plenty of fruit for pies and sauces. Be advised that buffaloberry is dioecious, meaning you must plant both male and female plants for a good yield.

Harvest buffaloberries after a light frost or two by placing a sheet on the ground and beating the bush with a rubber hose to loosen the fruit.

CHAPTER SEVEN

Annual Flowers

Growing annual flowers in Montana is a natural. Since their life cycles are completed in one gardening season, they will be up and growing quickly, filling in areas of the landscape that need a splash of color, or even an entire bed, and finishing before winter comes on. Interplant annuals in a perennial bed or among woody bushes. Or use them to replace and enhance early-blooming bulbs such as jonquils or tulips for continuous color.

Annuals are categorized by their relative resistance to frost and light freezes. Hardy annuals can withstand some frost, but not so with tender annuals! Half-hardy plants are somewhere in between. Some perennials are grown as annuals in Montana, and some of these may overwinter.

Selecting and Using Annuals

Remembering the color wheel will help when planning your annual bed. One year you may choose to use analogous colors in your scheme, such as red and yellow blanketflower (*Gaillardia*) with dwarf orange sunflowers (*Helianthus*), while the next year you may try a complementary color scheme by contrasting yellow marigolds (*Tagetes*) with blue lobelia (*Lobelia*). Select a single color for a bed that reads well from a distance, or use contrasting colors for interest. Warm colors like red, yellow, and orange appear to advance toward the viewer and stimulate the senses. Use these colors to attract attention to focal points in the yard. The cool colors (green, purple, and blue) are relaxing and tend to recede into the landscape. Petunias, snapdragons, and pansies are available in a wide range of colors and grow very well throughout the state.

Combining annuals with bulbs can give striking results. Try interplanting yellow daffodils or tulips with a sea of blue *Lobelia erinus* or purple sweet alyssum (*Lobularia maritima*).

Annuals work well in a perennial bed. If your bed will always be seen from a certain angle, graduate the plant heights. Use short moss rose (*Portulaca*), alyssum, petunias, or pansies in a border with taller perennials, annuals, or shrubs behind. Or use mid-height perennials with tall annuals, such as delphinium, calendula, or sunflowers behind. Take advantage of flower and foliage textures. Use feathery love-in-a-mist (*Nigella*) with bold sweet pea (*Lathyrus*), or plant smooth-petaled California poppy (*Eschscholzia californica*) with fluffy alyssum.

Plant heavenly scented annuals where you can enjoy their fragrance. Many annuals are at their best when massed. A single cluster of sweet alyssum may brighten up a spot, but when massed in a fragrant edging the flowers make more of a statement. Different varieties of pinks (*Dianthus*) massed are an olfactory knock-out. Petunias' bold statement becomes even bolder if they are planted where their fragrance can be enjoyed.

Transplants and Seedlings

Most Montanans purchase transplants at their local garden center in four- or six-packs. Look for stocky plants that are not root bound. Many annuals may be direct seeded to the garden. Or you may decide to try growing your own transplants indoors. Look on the seed packet for the number of days from seeding to bloom to determine if your growing season is long enough to direct sow or if you need to start your seeds indoors early. Then, knowing your average date of last spring frost, count back about eight weeks and start your transplants at that time. For most of the western part of the state, start your seeds around April 1. March 15 is better for gardeners in eastern Montana.

Use a soilless potting mix or a homemade media containing 50 percent soil, 25 percent peat moss, and 25 percent coarse sand. The soil-based media must be sterilized by placing it in trays or on cookie sheets in your oven, set to 180 degrees Fahrenheit. Monitor the soil temperature using a probe-type thermometer and, after the soil has reached 180 degrees, cook it for thirty minutes. This can be a smelly business, but it works well.

Cool the soil, screen out large pieces, and fill your pots or flats. Scatter seeds according to packet directions and cover with a depth of soil or sand twice the largest diameter of the seed. Be sure to label your pots! Keep humidity high by covering the pots with plastic wrap and keep temperatures generally between 50 and 80 degrees.

It's a good idea to bottom water seeded pots so the seeds and small seedlings aren't washed away or otherwise damaged. Place your pots in shallow trays of water for this.

You will need to supply supplemental light to your seedlings as they grow. Plants grown with too little light (or the wrong kind of light) become etiolated, leggy, and soft. Use a fluorescent fixture with one warm bulb and one cool bulb and keep the fixture just above the tops of the plants as they grow.

Transplant seedlings into individual containers when they have two to three true leaves.

Harden all transplants—whether purchased or grown at home—before setting them into the garden by placing them outside for short periods of time over a one- to two-week period. Increase the amount of time the plants are exposed to outdoor conditions each day. This will toughen them so they won't have such a shock coming out of ideal conditions into the intense Montana sunshine and cool nights. Set transplants of hardy annuals to the garden after the danger of hard frost has passed, and set those of half-hardy annuals about the time of the average date of last frost. Set transplants of tender annuals to the garden when the soil has warmed, or about two weeks after the average date of last frost.

Setting Plants in the Ground

Before planting, spread onto your bed an inch of compost and a complete fertilizer at the rate of a quarter pound of actual nitrogen per 100 square feet. For example, if you use a 5-10-10 fertilizer, apply 5 pounds per 100 square feet. Also apply amendments as needed to improve your soil structure (see chapter 1 for details). Careful attention to fertility now will give bountiful returns later in the summer.

Plant in the afternoon or on a cloudy day. Fluff up the rootball to encourage the roots to spread more easily. Space your plants according to the directions found on the seed pack, on the plant label that came with your transplants, or from a reference book. If you direct seeded your plants, they may become too crowded; don't forget to thin them!

Remove weeds that may have grown up and mulch with bark or even grass clippings to keep the soil cool and moist and to inhibit weed seed germination. You may also use landscape cloth to reduce the weed pressure. Landscape cloth is placed after thorough soil preparation and remains for the life of the cloth, often many years. Careful planning is required for plant placement, as you will be cutting slits in the fabric to place your plants. Cover your landscape cloth with an attractive bark mulch to finish the picture.

Maintenance

Annuals are fairly carefree. Keep the top 6 inches of soil moist. Drip or other emitter-type sprinklers work well in an annual bed. Give plants a little fertilizer weekly to keep them growing robustly.

To ensure continuous bloom, remove spent flowers so the plant works on making more flowers, not seeds. Seed formation and ripening tend to shut down plant growth and bloom. If you decide to save seed for next year's annuals, save them only from heirloom or other open-pollinated plants, since seeds from hybrid plants will not come true to type next year.

Clean up the flower beds after the killing frost. Leaving dead plants in your garden over winter will encourage disease organisms and insects to remain along with them. Some species will self-sow. If you want to allow your plants to go to seed, leave them in place until the seed heads are empty, then remove the plants.

Annual Flowers for Montana Gardens

These annuals are best bets for Montana summers. We indicate light needs or preferences, hardiness, height ranges, bloom time, and any special features or considerations.

African daisy (*Arctotis* spp.). Full sun; half-hardy; 12 to 30 inches. Blooms July to August. Won't flower when nights are hot.

Ageratum (*Ageratum* spp.). Full sun, tolerates partial shade; tender; 3 to 10 inches. Blooms July to September. Attracts butterflies.

Annual larkspur (*Consolida ambigua*). Full sun to partial shade; tender; 12 to 36 inches. Blooms July to August. Tolerates alkaline conditions.

Bachelor's buttons (*Centaurea cyanus*). Full sun, hardy; 12 to 18 inches. Blooms late spring to early summer. Cool nights are needed for flowering. Self-sows, hard to kill.

Calendula (*Calendula officinalis*). Full sun to partial shade; half-hardy; 18 to 36 inches. Blooms July to autumn. This cold-hardy plant is good for mountain gardens.

California poppy (*Eschscholzia californica*). Full sun; hardy; 12 to 18 inches. Blooms in summer. Self-sows. Likes light, sandy soil; good for mountain gardens.

Candytuft (*Iberis umbellata*). Full sun to partial shade; hardy; 10 inches. Blooms summer to fall. Prefers well-drained soil.

China aster (*Callistephus chinensis*). Full sun, tolerates partial shade; tender; 6 to 30 inches. Blooms August to September. Prefers cool nights. Thrives in fairly alkaline soils.

Clarkia (*Clarkia* spp.). Full sun, tolerates partial shade; hardy; 12 to 36 inches. Blooms June to July. Prefers cool nights.

Cleome (*Cleome hasslerana*). Full sun, tolerates partial shade; half-hardy; 36 to 72 inches. Blooms July to August. Subject to flea beetle.

Cosmos (*Cosmos* spp.). Full sun; half-hardy; 30 to 48 inches. Blooms summer to early fall. Prefers low fertility; do not overfertilize.

Four-o'clock (*Mirabilis jalapa*). Full sun, tolerates partial shade; hardy; 36 inches. Blooms midsummer to frost. Tolerates alkaline conditions.

Gaillardia or blanketflower (*Gaillardia* spp.). Full sun; hardy; 24 inches. Blooms July to frost. Self-sows. Good for mountain gardens.

Globe amaranth (*Gomphrena globosa*). Full sun; tender; 12 to 24 inches. Blooms summer to fall. Needs minimal water.

Impatiens (*Impatiens* spp.). Partial shade; tender; 18 inches. Blooms spring to late fall. Not drought resistant.

Lobelia (*Lobelia erinus*). Full sun to partial shade; half-hardy; 6 to 8 inches. Blooms continuously all season. Not heat resistant.

Love-in-a-mist (*Nigella damascena*). Full sun; hardy; 12 to 24 inches. Blooms all summer. Self-sows.

Marigold (*Tagetes* spp.). Full sun; half-hardy; 6 to 36 inches. Blooms midsummer to frost. Drought tolerant; good for mountain gardens.

Moss rose (*Portulaca grandiflora*). Full sun; tender; 4 inches. Blooms late spring. Self-sows. Drought tolerant.

Nasturtium (*Tropaeolum* spp.). Full sun, tolerates partial shade; half-hardy; 12 to 15 inches. Blooms midsummer. Don't overfertilize.

Pansy (*Viola wittrockiana*). Full sun; hardy; 5 to 12 inches. Blooms early spring to late fall. Can self-sow. Tender perennial; good for mountain gardens.

Petunia (*Petunia* spp.). Full sun; half-hardy; 8 to 24 inches. Blooms early summer to late fall. Very adaptable, several types; good for mountain gardens.

Poppy (*Papaver* spp.). Full sun; hardy; 12 to 36 inches. Blooms late spring. Self-sows and crosses; good for mountain gardens.

Salvia (*Salvia* spp.). Full sun, tolerates partial shade; tender; 8 inches to 4 feet. Many species, forms, and colors.

Snapdragon (*Antirrhinum* spp.). Full sun; hardy; 6 to 24 inches. Blooms July to frost. Many F1 hybrids available.

Sunflower (*Helianthus* spp.). Full sun; half-hardy; 16 inches to 15 feet. Blooms midsummer to frost. Dwarf forms are good for small properties.

Sweet alyssum (*Lobularia maritima*). Full sun to partial shade; hardy; 3 to 12 inches. Blooms June to September. Self-sows. Adaptable.

Sweet pea (*Lathyrus odoratus*). Full sun, tolerates partial shade; hardy; 24 to 48 inches. Blooms summer to fall. Needs cool, moist climate.

Verbena (*Verbena* spp.). Full sun; tender; 8 inches to 5 feet. Blooms all summer. Attracts butterflies.

Herbaceous Perennials, Bulbs, and Roses

Montana gardeners love their bulbs, roses, and perennials—plants considered by many to be the backbone of a flower bed. Like friends returning from the holidays, gardeners welcome these plants' return each spring. One of the biggest challenges we face is in the selection process. Some perennials that have been designated a noxious weed by individual counties are nonetheless sold by catalogs and nurseries. To be sure your selections are not designated "weeds," contact your local Weed Control District or MSU Extension Office. In addition, many cultivars are not adapted to Montana conditions, yet they are still sold in the state. Nonadapted species selected by ill-informed gardeners will be great disappointments. Here's the information you need to select appropriate plants for your garden!

Herbaceous Perennials

Unlike annuals, well-cared-for herbaceous perennials faithfully return year after year, bringing their unique charm to the garden. There is a perennial plant that will thrive in just about any Montana garden; you just need to place the right plant in the right spot.

Unlike woody perennial shrubs discussed in the next chapter, herbaceous perennials die to the ground every fall and grow a new top each spring. They can be planted in fall or spring, but fall planting is usually best.

Some perennials aren't fussy, but others have specific soil requirements, so choose your plants with care and prepare the soil well prior to planting. Chapter 1 can help you start your soil right. Most perennials do best in a loamy soil that is well drained and high in organic matter with plenty of nitrogen and phosphorus added. Dig your planting hole twice as deep as the rootball is high, then backfill with loose soil to encourage deep rooting. Most perennials do best at a neutral soil pH, but some,

Biennial versus Perennial

Biennials are often confused with herbaceous perennials. Both commonly die to the ground during the winter. While perennials grow an entire new top and flower each year for many years, biennials produce a rosette of leaves their first year, flower the second year, then die. Biennials commonly grown in Montana include campanula, hollyhocks, and phlox.

Critter Fitters

- Perennials and biennials that attract hummingbirds: bee balm, bellflower, bleeding heart, columbine, daylily, hollyhock
- Perennials and biennials that attract butterflies and bees: bee balm, black-eyed Susan, common yarrow, daylily, gayfeather
- Perennials and biennials that are resistant to deer and rabbits: black-eyed Susan, bleeding heart, columbine, common yarrow, daylily (rabbits only!), iris

like irises (*Iris*) and baby's breath (*Gypsophila*), perform well in alkaline soils.

In spring press perennials back into their places if they have frost heaved. Apply a complete fertilizer such as 10-10-10 or 5-10-10 when spring growth starts at the rate of about two pounds per 100 square feet. Fertilize only once more in early summer, around Father's Day. Mulch perennials with compost or rotted manure in the fall after the plant has died back to both protect the crown and roots and to provide valuable nutrients for the following growing season.

Water the plants well, keeping the soil moist to a depth of about a foot.

Many perennials require staking to support their long stems and flower spikes, particularly in windy areas. Bamboo stakes are readily available, and heavy-flowered plants with weak stalks such as peonies may be supported by specially made wire cages or even with tomato cages. Tying stems too tightly to stakes will result in damage to your plants, so loosely tie them, using a soft wide band or baler twine. Be sure you use a twine that will not disintegrate easily.

Deadheading the plants in fall not only tidies the perennial bed but also allows the plants to better utilize their resources to prepare for the winter and next year's growth instead of setting seed.

Many perennial varieties will not set viable seed due to extensive domestication and hybridization, so propagation must be accomplished by crown division. Divide your perennials every couple of years to improve bloom, reduce crowding, and supply your friends with plants. Divide in fall or early spring when the plant is dormant, though fall is the preferred season. Dig up the plant and work compost or well-rotted manure into the hole. Divide the plant with a shovel or your hands and reset the pieces into their new locations and water well to expel any pockets of air in the soil.

Many perennials are long-lived, but some die after only a few years. Common yarrow (*Achillea millefolium*), gayfeather (*Liatris* spp.), iris, and garden phlox (*Phlox paniculata*) live for many years, while blue flax (*Linum perenne*), columbines (*Aquilegia* spp.), and delphiniums (*Delphinium* spp.) often die after several years. Long-lived perennials may be divided every year to keep blooms at their best.

Great Perennials for Montana Gardens

These perennials are proven plants for Montana gardens. We indicate light needs or preferences, height ranges, bloomtime, and any special features or considerations.

Baby's breath (*Gypsophila paniculata*). Full sun; 24 to 30 inches. Blooms late July. Prefers slightly alkaline soils.

Bee balm (*Monarda fistulosa*). Part shade to full shade; 24 to 48 inches. Blooms in summer. Attracts birds and butterflies.

Bellflower (*Campanula medium*). Full sun, tolerates partial shade; 24 to 36 inches. Blooms early summer. Bellflower is a biennial. It's also known as Canterbury bells.

Black-eyed Susan (*Rudbeckia fulgida*). Full sun to partial shade; 24 to 48 inches. Blooms in summer. Looks great planted in masses.

Bleeding heart (*Dicentra spectabilis*). Light shade to partial shade; 24 to 36 inches. Blooms spring and summer. Will die back in dry summers but comes back. Suitable for mountain gardens.

Blue flax (*Linum perenne*). Full sun; 12 to 18 inches. Blooms midsummer. Ephemeral flowers. Suitable for mountain gardens.

Columbine (*Aquilegia* spp.). Part shade; 24 to 36 inches. Blooms spring and summer. Leaf miners are a problem. Suitable for mountain gardens.

Common yarrow (*Achillea millefolium*). Full sun to partial shade; 12 to 24 inches. Blooms spring and summer. Resistant to deer browse. Suitable for mountain gardens.

Coralbells (*Heuchera sanguinea*). Light shade to partial shade;

6 to 18 inches. Flowers in summer to late summer. Good in a shady, dry spot.

Daylily (*Hemerocallis* spp.). Full sun to light shade; 12 to 36 inches. Flowers spring and summer. Divide every two to three years for best results.

Delphinium or **larkspur** (*Delphinium* spp.). Full sun; 36 to 72 inches. Blooms early summer. Excellent for mountain gardens. Short lived.

Gayfeather (*Liatris* spp.). Full sun; 18 to 36 inches. Flowers late summer. Attracts butterflies.

Globeflower (*Trollius asiaticus*). Partial shade; 18 to 24 inches. Blooms early summer. Prefers cool, moist soil.

Hollyhock (*Alcea* spp.). Full sun, tolerates partial shade; 5 to 8 feet. Blooms in summer. Biennial. Suitable for mountain gardens.

Iris (*Iris* spp.). Full sun, tolerates partial shade; 8 to 48 inches. Blooms late spring to early summer. Prefers slightly alkaline soils. Suitable for mountain gardens.

Lily-of-the-valley (*Convallaria majalis*). Full sun to shade; 6 to 12 inches. Flowers early summer. Multiplies rapidly, so thin often.

Lupine (*Lupinus* spp.). Full sun to partial shade; 12 to 36 inches. Blooms in July. Russell hybrids are popular. Suitable for mountain gardens.

Penstemon or **beardtongue** (*Penstemon* spp.). Full sun, tolerates partial shade; 8 to 24 inches. Blooms late summer to early fall. Attracts birds and butterflies.

Peony (*Paeonia* spp.). Full sun, tolerates partial shade; 24 to 36 inches. Blooms late spring to early summer. Cover tuberous roots with at most 1 to 2 inches of soil. Suitable for mountain gardens.

Phlox, garden (*Phlox paniculata*). Full sun to partial shade; 24 to 36 inches. Blooms in summer. Many species and varieties. Suitable for mountain gardens.

Pinks (*Dianthus* spp.). Full sun, tolerates partial shade; 8 to 12 inches. Blooms late June to August. Many popular varieties. Suitable for mountain gardens, though some may not overwinter.

Prairie coneflower (*Echinacea* spp.). Full sun, 24 to 36 inches. Blooms midsummer to fall. *E. angustifolia* is native to Montana.

Primrose (*Primula polyantha*). Sun to partial shade; 6 to 12 inches. Blooms early summer. Remove dead foliage in fall.

Sedum (*Sedum* spp.). Full sun, tolerates partial shade; 2 to 24 inches. Blooms in summer. Includes ground covers and uprights. Suitable for mountain gardens.

Shasta daisy (*Chrysanthemum x superbum*). Full sun; 24 inches. Blooms mid- to late summer. May become invasive on good sites. Suitable for mountain gardens.

Bulbs for Montana Gardens

What a thrill, after a long bleak winter, to venture into the yard to see crocus flowers popping up through the snow. Nothing says spring like bulbs, and they grow very well in Montana! Hardy bulbs will overwinter just fine; tender bulbs will have to be dug in autumn and stored for replanting the following spring.

When novice gardeners hear the word *bulbs,* they automatically think of the "Dutch" bulbs—hyacinths, daffodils, tulips, and crocus, none of which originated in Holland. But there are many more, sometimes unfortunately called the "minor" bulbs. The crown imperial, or *Fritillaria imperialis,* is a good example. We've seen this eye-catching plant take hard spring frost after hard frost, only to continue on to glorious early-season bloom!

Bulbs are wonderful for naturalizing. Plant spring-flowering bulbs in the autumn around mid- to late September, and plant fall-flowering bulbs in spring.

Purchase your bulbs from a reputable company. Prepare your soil deeply, as you would for a perennial bed, then cast the bulbs into the bed, planting them where they land for a natural effect. Locate spring bulbs beneath deciduous trees that provide light

Bulb Tidbits

- All true bulbs have deep root systems. The roots and the tops die each year and the bulb goes completely dormant before regrowth in the spring.

- Plant spring bulbs around Labor Day and certainly before Columbus Day. But if you forgot to plant the bulbs until around Thanksgiving, plant them anyway and take a chance. If you wait until spring, your bulbs will have a poor chance of growing.

shade. This allows the bulb flowers to bloom in full sunlight before the full tree canopy develops. The tree then shades the bulb leaves slightly, keeping them cooler so that they will produce food over a long period of time. This promotes healthier, more long-lived, and deeper-rooted bulbs.

Planting depths for bulbs are often given in fancy and hard-to-understand charts. Remember that the depth is measured from the top of the bulb to the soil surface. In Montana you must modify the recommended planting depth based on the characteristics of your soil, planting slightly less deeply in heavy soils or on

The Bonemeal Myth

For a long time gardeners mixed bonemeal into the bulb planting hole with the understanding that the phosphorus promoted root growth specifically. It doesn't. While the bonemeal won't harm anything, it won't do much for the bulbs. In our alkaline soils it takes about eight years for the phosphorus in bonemeal to become available to the plant roots. The phosphorus in a complete fertilizer would become available much sooner.

north exposures and slightly more deeply in sandy soils or on south exposures.

Care after bloom: The bulbs depend upon their leaves to replenish the carbohydrates they used to push their flower growth and to provide nutrients for next year's. Never remove foliage prematurely; always leave it in place until leaf color fades to a yellowish green and the leaves begin to shrivel. Then it is safe to remove the foliage to tidy the area.

Transplanting: After several years your bulb plantings may become overcrowded, leading to smaller flowers or, perhaps, all leaves and no flowers at all. If this is the case in your garden, divide the bulbs as soon as the foliage has died down completely but before it has fallen off (which makes the bulbs difficult to locate).

Air-dry the bulbs, store them in a dark, cool place, and replant them in the autumn in well-prepared beds.

Best Bulbs for Montana

Here are some of the best bulbs for Big Sky Country. We list light preferences, height, planting depth, bloom time, and cultivation tips or comments.

Allium (*Allium* spp.). Full sun; 24 inches. Plant *A. giganteum* 7 inches deep; 5 inches for other species. Blooms late spring to summer, depending on species. Flowers have interesting shapes.

Crocus (*Crocus* spp.). Full sun to partial shade; 2 to 6 inches. Plant 4 inches deep. Blooms early spring. Will bloom through snow cover.

Daffodil (*Narcissus* spp.). Full sun to partial shade; 4 to 24 inches. Plant 6 to 8 inches deep. Blooms in spring. Deer and vole resistant.

Fritillary, crown imperial (*Fritillaria imperialis*). Light shade; 3 to 4 inches. Plant 9 inches deep. Blooms in spring. Unusually striking in the garden; skunklike odor.

Gladiolus (*Gladiolus* spp.). Full sun to partial shade; 18 to 48 inches. Plant 4 to 6 inches deep. Blooms late summer. Grown as annuals; dig when foliage dies in fall and store between 35 and 50 degrees Fahrenheit. Support in windy areas.

Glory-of-the-snow (*Chionodoxa* spp.). Full sun; 3 inches. Plant 3 inches deep. Blooms in spring, as snow melts. Blue flowers contrast beautifully with snow.

Grape hyacinth (*Muscari* spp.). Full sun to partial shade; 6 to 10 inches. Plant 4 inches deep. Blooms in early spring. Plant in lawn areas.

Hyacinth (*Hyacinthus* spp.). Full sun to light shade; 8 inches. Plant 5 inches deep. Blooms in spring. Very fragrant.

Snowdrop (*Galanthus* spp.). Light shade; 3 inches. Plant 3 to 4 inches deep. Blooms in early spring. White flowers.

Squill (*Scilla* spp.). Light shade; 4 inches. Plant 3 inches deep. Blooms in early spring. Blue flowers. *S. campanulata* blooms in summer in white, pink, and blue.

Tulip (*Tulipa* spp.). Full sun; 6 to 14 inches. Plant 8 to 10 inches deep. Blooms in spring. Deer food. Deeper planting depths give bulbs longer life.

Roses for Montana

Everyone loves roses, but growing them in Montana can be problematic. It is beyond the scope of this book to discuss all the rose types, most of which will not grow in our state. However, some varieties of a few types will make it quite well in the warmer areas, and most varieties of one type will make it across nearly the entire state.

Learn the types of roses before you order your plants. The tea roses certainly are not well adapted to most of Montana; neither are most polyanthas, floribundas, grandifloras, and hybrid teas. Some climbing roses like 'Blaze' are cold hardy here, but their being off the ground and exposed to bright winter sun and drying winds makes growing them in all but the most protected gardens a real challenge. 'Coral Dawn' may survive in protected gardens. Trailing roses make long canes that trail and spread over banks and walls. Try 'Max Graf' in the warmer parts of the state. While some miniature roses may be cold hardy in protected gardens, they will mat beneath snow and likely succumb to disease and voles.

Hybrid tea roses are the darlings of gardeners, but they are not particularly cold hardy, nor pest resistant, and they are pretty finicky about their soil and culture. Gardeners who are successful with this type of rose live in the warmer parts of the state and generally have highly protected gardens and good soil. In other words, they have wonderful microclimates, and their roses, like the old 'Mister Lincoln', 'Chrysler Imperial', and 'Tropicana', survive for many years. Some Montana gardeners who love hybrid tea roses but live in harsher areas decide to bite the bullet and grow them as expensive annuals. Gardeners wanting to make a longer-term investment choose to grow shrub roses.

Shrub roses are hardy, pest resistant, and as a group perhaps the roses best adapted to Montana. Hybrids of *Rosa rugosa*, the rugosa rose, are particularly tolerant of cold, poor soil, and dry conditions. Shrub roses make beautiful specimen or accent plants and will grow into dense bushes. Height will vary with variety and soil, but they all require little care, remaining hardy and vigorous for many years. Shrub roses in general are closer to their species type and are less refined than the hybrid teas. That makes them generally hardier and more pest resistant. And through the efforts of modern plant breeders, the flowers of the shrub roses are just as impressive as those of the hybrid teas.

Purchase your rosebushes locally and plant them as soon as the ground can be worked in early spring. Plants grown in southern nurseries will not be as cold hardy as those grown in the north, even though they are the same variety. Be sure to plant your roses when they are still dormant. This is especially important if you have purchased bare-root plants.

Roses need six to eight hours of sunlight per day, preferably with morning sun exposure. The blasting afternoon Montana sun will fade rose color from red to pink and from yellow to white. Morning shade may encourage the development of fungal diseases, like blackspot, since the leaves retain dew longer.

Roses do not tolerate wet feet. Before planting, work coarse gravel and compost into poorly drained soils, or add compost into soils already well drained. A soil pH of 6.5 to 7.0 is best. If you plant roses where the soil has a pH near 8.0, the leaves will become chlorotic (yellow). Interveinal chlorosis indicates an iron deficiency induced by high soil pH.

Prepare the planting hole as you would for other perennials, working the soil to a depth of at least 2 feet. Trim away any dead, diseased, or injured roots or canes and cut remaining canes back to about a foot in height. Trim long roots to fit the hole. If you spiral them into the hole to make them fit, they will continue to grow in a circling manner and eventually girdle the plant. Don't do it!

If your roses have been grafted, set plants with the bud union about 2 inches below the soil surface. Spread the roots so they slope naturally, taking care not to break them. Fill the hole and firm the soil around the roots as you go. When you have replaced half the soil, fill the planting hole with water and allow it to soak in, then fill the hole with the remainder of the soil, and soak again. Mound the plant with 6 to 8 inches of soil to protect it from late frost. Remove this extra soil after the danger of frost has passed. Do not apply fertilizer the year you plant.

Soak the soil around roses once a week but keep the foliage dry. Each spring after planting, apply a complete fertilizer, like 10-10-10 or 5-10-10, at the rate of three pounds per 100 square feet over two applications, with half applied as new growth approaches 2 inches in length and the rest around Father's Day. Do not fertilize roses after July 4 in Montana.

Keep your plants attractive by pruning out dead, diseased, or overlapping branches. Deadhead your young roses to allow your plant to provide nutrition to the leaves and roots rather than formation of fruits. When your shrub rose has become established (after the third year), leave the flowers to form attractive hips.

Sometimes long, vigorous shoots arise from below the graft union of grafted roses. They are often a slightly different color than the top of the bush and may have seven leaflets rather than the more normal five found on most rose varieties. Remove all of these shoots as soon as you see them. They are from the rootstock and will produce inferior roses far different from the variety you planted.

Rose pests. Powdery mildew, blackspot, and rust are problems on Montana roses, especially where air drainage is poor. Keep the foliage dry at all times. Use a fungicide to control the diseases in severe cases.

Winter protection. Established shrub roses usually need no winter protection. For young shrub roses and all hybrid tea roses, however, erect a small windbreak and sunscreen on their west sides. Mound soil about 8 to 10 inches around the crown of hybrid teas to further protect the graft union and crown area against cold. It is always a good idea to mound snow over roses whenever possible, keeping it fluffy to provide good insulation during the winter. A crust of ice spells doom to roses; break it up whenever it occurs, usually in late winter.

Good Shrub Roses for Montana Gardens

'**Austrian Copper**' (*R. foetida* var. *bicolor*). Single flowers are copper above, yellow beneath. Color is variable and unstable.

'**Champlain**' (Explorer series). Red semidouble flowers. Sprouts easily from crown after winter damage.

'**Cuthbert Grant**' (Parkland series). Red semidouble flowers. Repeat bloomer; fragrant.

'**Grootendorst Supreme**' (*R. rugosa* hybrid). Red, double, pinked delicate flowers resemble carnations.

'**Hansa**' (*R. rugosa* hybrid). Mauve to red or purple, clove-scented flowers. Very hardy, with large hips.

'**Harison Yellow**' (*R. foetida* hybrid). Bright yellow. Feathery foliage.

'**Henry Hudson**' (Explorer series). White, semidouble, clove-scented flowers.

'**Jens Munk**' (Explorer series). Pink flowers. Repeat bloomer, viciously thorny.

'**John Cabot**' (Explorer series). Reddish purple flowers, repeat bloomer.

'**Morden Blush**' (Parkland series). Light pink, tea-scented flowers.

'**Morden Sunrise**' (Parkland series). Lightly scented yellow, semidouble flowers.

Red-leaved rose (*R. glauca*). Mauve pink, unusual five-petaled flower. Robust grower; plant it where it can sprawl.

'**Therese Bugnet**' (*R. rugosa* hybrid). Pink double flowers. Can be damaged by some fungicides. Canes nearly thornless; does not tolerate wind.

CHAPTER NINE

Trees and Shrubs

When selecting a tree or shrub, gardeners most commonly ask how fast it will grow, how tall and wide it will get, and what pests will attack it. There are too many variables for a quick answer. The species and variety, soil type, fertilization schedule, moisture availability, and site (wind, growing season, and whether you are planting in eastern or western Montana) all play a part in the correct response.

But let's clear up one thing right now. Rate of growth is relative; there are no really fast-growing trees and shrubs in Montana, only those that grow *relatively* fast. And in general trees that grow relatively fast tend to live short lives (twenty to thirty years) and be weak wooded, often splitting or snapping off near the tops. Also, the heights and spreads commonly given for plants in those general gardening books for the most part do not apply to Montana conditions. Figure that, in general, plants will take longer to grow here and their mature heights and spreads will be less than indicated in those tables, thanks to our difficult conditions.

Make your selections based upon hardiness zones, soil types, winds, and the relative presence of chinooks and upon recommendations in *Tree and Shrub Selection Guide* (MSU Extension Bulletin EB 123 rev.). Then give the plants proper care and relax for a decade until they begin to take shape.

Purchasing Trees and Shrubs

Plant survival is at the top of everyone's mind, and a key to high-survival rates is to plant the right plants in the right place at the right time. Those deals of twenty-five plants for $5 are just not worth it. Most of those plants are no more than rooted cuttings, and you will be lucky if one in five survives the first year. Aside from the end-of-season sales that many nurseries hold, there are no deals in purchasing plants. Spend the money . . . it will be your smallest investment. You get what you pay for.

Many folks like to go into the hills to dig out wild plants and move them to the yard. Don't do it. Those plants may not be adapted to your conditions even though they may be growing only a few miles from your mailbox. Wild plants also tend to have scraggly root systems, and you cannot count on digging enough of the roots along with the top of the plant to ensure a successful transplant. Removing plants from the wild also leaves a previously occupied niche open for invasive species to move in. Lastly, you may be breaking the law in digging plants from private or government property. In an effort to save money, you will spend lots of it on gasoline and perhaps fines.

Purchase from local nurseries and garden centers whenever possible. They are highly likely to have species and varieties especially adapted to Montana, and you get great satisfaction from supporting a local business. Large chain stores are apt to carry some species that are not adapted to Montana. Decide what you want to buy before you shop and don't be led astray by the advertisements.

But just because a local store offers a plant for sale does not guarantee it will grow well for you. Ask the sales clerk if the stock was propagated from northern-grown plants. It is well known that a tree of a certain species propagated from southern nursery stock will not be quite as hardy or as well adapted to northern gardens as one of the same species propagated from northern

The Right Root-ball

A tree should have a root-ball about 1 foot in diameter for every inch of trunk caliper. A tree having proportionately less of a root-ball may suffer greater transplant shock and have a greater chance of dying soon after planting. Trees larger than a 2-inch caliper are difficult to handle without special equipment because of their greater height, weight, and the size of their root-ball.

stock. If you have two northern sources—often Oregon and Minnesota—choose plants from Minnesota, since its climate more closely resembles Montana's.

Many novices want to plant the largest tree they can find, expecting to get an "instant" landscape. That is the wrong thing to do. It is expensive to plant very large trees and shrubs, and large plants suffer far more from transplant shock than smaller specimens. You're better off to select a smaller tree or shrub that recovers faster from transplanting and is far less expensive to purchase and transplant.

What is the right size? Evergreen trees between 3 and 6 feet tall are the best size for transplanting. Select deciduous trees with a 1-inch caliper measured about a foot above the top of the soil line. These will be about 6 to 8 feet in height, and one person can maneuver the plants fairly easily. A tree with a 2-inch caliper may be 10 to 12 feet tall and will be far more difficult to handle.

Improperly moving your plants from the nursery to the yard can be fatal. Carry your plants by their root-balls, not by the canes or the trunk. If you sit a small, unprotected tree in full leaf in the back of a pickup truck, or extend it from the trunk of your car, and then drive 70 miles per hour from the nursery to your home, you will scorch the leaves, set the tree back, and may kill it outright. Sometimes it will take a few weeks for this damage to become fully apparent. In the cases of fall planting, the plants may have shed their leaves before the damage is noticed, and in the spring you might blame the plant's death on winter damage—but you killed it before it got home. The proper way to transport a tree is to lay the tree down, wrap the branches in burlap or cover the bed of the pickup with a tarp, then drive slowly home. In short, protect the top and the root-ball of the plant from windburn.

Proper Planting

Trees and shrubs come as bare-root, balled-and-burlapped, and container plants. Bare-root plants must be transplanted when they are dormant, which limits planting to early spring and to late fall. Container plants can be transplanted anytime the ground is not frozen, but they have better survival rates if transplanted in the cool early spring or between Labor Day and Columbus Day. Balled-and-burlapped plants are best transplanted at that time as well.

Try to plant when environmental stresses are minimal. That's why fall planting between Labor Day and Columbus Day is very good. Plants need at least a month to begin to spread their roots into the soil. Since the soil freezes by about mid-November, it's a good idea not to plant anything after mid-October, or about Columbus Day. Soil freezes will contribute to frost heaving and severe winter desiccation in late-planted trees. Early spring is the next best time to transplant trees and shrubs. Do this when the soil temperature at an 8-

How Closely to Plant Trees?

To figure how closely to plant two trees, average their mature spreads. For example, a tree with a mature spread of 30 feet and one with a mature spread of 20 feet should be spaced at least 25 feet apart.

inch depth has reached about 40 to 45 degrees Fahrenheit. The precise date varies across the state but usually falls sometime in April.

People crowd young plants, forgetting that small plants become big plants someday. You may wind up with a jungle or painfully have to remove every other plant to make room. Consider the location before you dig a hole and plunk a tree into it. To see what the view from your living room window will be with the full-grown tree in place, get a long pole the length of the approximate mature height of the tree and stick it in the planting hole. Does the pole block a beautiful view? Will it cause too much shade in summer? Is the tree too close to the house? If all looks fine, proceed with the hole.

Fertilizer-Free Zone

Do not place fertilizers in a tree or shrub's planting hole. To our knowledge there is no reliable science-based evidence that "root enhancers," "root hormones," or vitamins are in any way beneficial in transplanting woody plants.

Dig a hole about half again as deep and as wide as the root-ball and fill it with water at suppertime. If water remains in the hole after breakfast the next morning, the soil is too poorly drained for most plants. Select an alternate site.

Carefully set the plant in the hole as deep as it grew in the nursery and without breaking the root-ball. Position the plant so that its most attractive side shows. If you live in a windy area, set the plant so that its lowest branch is to windward. Remove plastic, metal, and cardboard containers. If your plant came in a wire basket, snip the top couple of rings of wire, but do not disturb the soil ball. You can leave burlap in place so long as you cut the bindings and loosen the top around the trunk. A collar of burlap that protrudes above the soil line will wick moisture away from the root zone. Cover that collar completely with soil.

Trim any overly long roots to fit the hole properly; do not wrap the roots around the ball to fit the hole. Roots wrapped into the hole will grow in a circling fashion and eventually girdle the tree. Backfill the hole with nothing but what came out of it, placing the topsoil in first and the subsoil on top. Fill the hole halfway with soil and flood it. When the water has drained, fill the rest of the way and flood it once again to settle the soil about the roots.

Many trees were crowded in the nursery and may be tall and lanky. These require staking for a year or two. Place the stakes at planting time so as not to damage the roots once they establish.

Because of the intense Montana sun, it is important to wrap the trunks of all young deciduous trees with burlap or tree wrap to protect against sunscald. For the first several years, wrap the

trunks of all trees in October up to the lowest branch and remove the wrap in April. Do not leave the wrap on all season long. Continue to protect the trunks on older trees if those species have dark-colored bark, such as cherry and apple. You can also protect tree trunks from sunscald by painting them up to the lowest branches with white interior latex paint. Deciduous shrubs and evergreens are not subject to severe sunscald and need no trunk wraps.

After setting the plant in its new home, prune out any damaged branches and any low-hanging branches, then hang up the pruning tools. The old recommendation of removing a third of the top of the plant is out of favor. Remove dead branches as they develop, but otherwise leave the plant alone.

Mulching is a good practice in Montana. Use organic mulch such as wood chips or bark or a crushed stone mulch with a landscape fabric underlayment. If you use organic mulch, keep it 2 inches away from the trunk or canes to reduce vole damage in winter.

Fertilizing Established Plants

Soil tests do not accurately indicate the nutrient needs of trees and shrubs in Montana landscapes. We know that nitrogen is the nutrient most often lacking, so examine the plants themselves to see if they need fertilizer. Woody broadleaf plants that lack nitrogen will have uniform yellow green leaves, particularly on the lower limbs. The leaves will be small and thin and develop bright fall color before dropping early. Shoots will be short and thin and may have a reddish cast. Spring bloom may be heavy and late. On conifers the needles may be yellow, short, and spaced closely together. Needles may drop, and the lower parts of the plants may yellow while the top remains green.

Most of the time a tree or shrub planted in a lawn that receives regular fertilizing utilizes the nutrients that leach out of the grass root zone and rarely needs additional fertilizer. If you determine that your woody plants need nutrients, apply a complete fertilizer such as 16-16-16 in the autumn after the leaves drop but before Columbus Day at the rate of about one to two pounds of actual nitrogen per 1,000 square feet of dripline area. Special camellia and rhododendron-azalea fertilizers give an acid reaction, making them especially beneficial for acid-loving plants where soil pH is neutral or acid. However, don't expect the weak acid in this type of fertilizer to substantially lower pH in the soil volume of a Montana home landscape. Other fertilizers packaged for certain plants, such as vegetable garden fertilizer and rose fertilizer, do not have as valid a background of research. If the analyses of various fertilizers match and there are no specialty ingredients involved, then select the least expensive brand.

Watering

Give your trees and shrub sufficient water to keep the top 10 inches of soil moist. You might build a moat about your trees to hold the water, but be sure to kick a hole in it in the fall. Standing water in winter freezes and can damage the tree crown. When the leaves on deciduous trees have begun to fall, give all your landscape plants about 1 inch of water per week up until the time the soil freezes. Take advantage of any winter thaw by watering the soil once again. This is particularly important with evergreens.

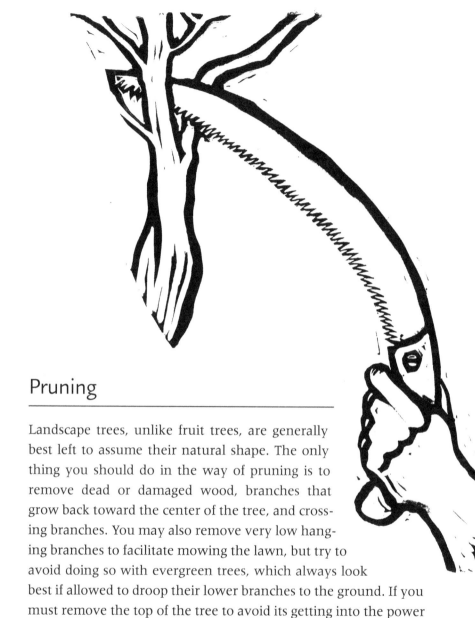

Pruning

Landscape trees, unlike fruit trees, are generally best left to assume their natural shape. The only thing you should do in the way of pruning is to remove dead or damaged wood, branches that grow back toward the center of the tree, and crossing branches. You may also remove very low hanging branches to facilitate mowing the lawn, but try to avoid doing so with evergreen trees, which always look best if allowed to droop their lower branches to the ground. If you must remove the top of the tree to avoid its getting into the power lines, you planted the wrong tree—its aesthetic value will be lost forever by the topping maneuver.

Most pruning is best done in the very early spring, before the buds swell. It's cooler then, more pleasant to work, there are few other chores to be done, and the lack of leaves lets you see the framework of the tree for better shaping. Some plants, such as the birches and walnuts, "bleed" profusely if pruned at this time of year. If it becomes a nuisance to deal with sap on the sidewalk, then prune in very late spring or early summer. Be advised, though, that the bleeding is only a nuisance and in no way damages the tree.

All shrubs send up suckers from their base as a way of rejuvenating themselves. There-fore, they all need annual pruning to remove the old wood and make room for the new. If your plant is a flow-ering shrub, it is especially important to remove the old wood routinely for the best flowers. Remove canes older than about five or six years and thin out those remaining so that about a dozen of the healthiest, youngest canes remain. Make your cuts at ground level. If you have the time, you may also thin out some of the shoots inside the bush, opening it up to air and sunlight. Shrubs that flower with or before the common lilac (*Syringa vulgaris*) are considered spring-flowering shrubs and generally should be pruned immedi-ately after their flowers fade. Shrubs that flower after the com-mon lilac (summer-flowering shrubs) are pruned in March.

Some hedge plants, such as caragana and lilac, may get over-grown. To rejuvenate them, cut them to the ground in early spring. Do this only on healthy plants that you can water and fer-tilize. Cutting the entire hedge at once is drastic, but it may work, although it causes a lot of whippy, "weedy" growth that must be thinned out. It's better to cut back a third of the hedge each year for three years. After cutting, give the plants a sprinkle of fertilizer and plenty of water and they will be back to "normal" in no time.

Perfect Pruning

For detailed accounts of pruning the trees and shrubs commonly found in the Montana landscapes, get a copy of *Tree and Shrub Grower's Guide*, published by Montana State University Extension Service.

Remember, this drastic approach works with caragana and lilac, but it does not work with all shrubs. Consult your local MSU Extension agent if you want to rejuvenate a species other than these two.

Troublesome Woody Plants

There are enough good plants for Montana landscapes without having to resort to using plants that can give you major trouble. All plants have their pros and cons, but here are a few with which to exercise caution.

Russian olive (*Eleagnus angustifolia*). This tree introduced from Siberia grows very well in most of Montana, although there are some places in eastern Montana where even this hardy plant will not survive. Unfortunately, on good sites Russian olive becomes invasive and can take over the landscape rapidly, crowd-

Plants and Leach Fields

We often get questions about which trees to plant near a leach field. Some species, such as the cottonwoods, willows, and maples, are notorious for getting their roots into the pipes and clogging the drainage. Certainly don't even think about planting those species within 100 feet of a leach field. But in general, all trees are opportunistic when it comes to foraging for water and nutrients, so it is best to plant *no* trees near the leach field. How far is "near"? Since tree roots can extend between one-and-a-half and two times the spread of the dripline, plant trees at a minimum of twice their mature spread from the leach field. It is better still if you can plant them farther away. Shrubs are not quite so bad at damaging leach fields; nonetheless, plant them no closer than twice their mature spread. Grass is the best plant to grow over a leach field.

ing out other species. This has happened north of Townsend and near Laurel, for example. There are far better plants for the landscape than Russian olive, such as those listed later in this chapter. Grow them if you can and leave Russian olive as a last resort.

Birch (*Betula* spp.). Birches are attractive, especially those with white bark and weeping branches. But birches need a good supply of water and are subject to attack by borers and leaf miners. During Montana's recent years of drought, birches have suffered mightily, some dying outright from dry conditions. Borers tend to attack trees in a weakened condition, and if the drought does not kill the birches, the borers do. Drought will come again, so think twice about planting this species.

Hybrid poplars (*Populus* spp.). These are relatively fast-growing trees and, as such, are weak wooded. They are also subject to borer infestation and gall-forming eriophyid mites. The galls formed by these mites are apple sized and detract from the attractiveness of the plants.

Aspen (*Populus tremuloides*). Folks enjoy the rustle of aspen leaves in autumn winds. The plants are native to Montana, well adapted to our conditions, and almost universally planted. As you consider planting aspens, remember that they are fast growing but weak wooded and short lived. They are subject to severe borer infestations, and they sucker badly. If we had a nickel for every time we were asked how to rid the plants of suckers, we'd be millionaires. The short answer is that you can't. It is in this plant's nature to

Cottonless Cottonwoods

The sexes are separate on cottonwood trees, and until they flower there is no way to tell the sex of field-run seedling cottonwoods. All-male clones do exist, the result of propagating male cottonwoods from cuttings. These are labeled "cottonless cottonwoods."

sucker and to form groves of trees. All you can do is mow or clip the suckers continuously, forever.

Cottonwoods (*Populus* spp.). These are majestic natives of Montana, reaching heights of up to 100 feet. But they need plenty of water, are weak wooded, and are prone to borer infestations. They sucker, and the females produce lots of "cotton," the feathery white tissue for seed dispersal. This kicks off the allergy season in grand style. If you have a small yard, if water is scarce, or if you are allergic to these plants, do not plant cottonwoods.

Trees and Shrubs That Work in Montana

Many trees and shrubs will not grow at all in Montana. Still others will grow but will struggle, never achieving their full beauty. That said, there are many woody plants that will take our conditions and give us all they have. The following is a partial list of hardy trees and shrubs that will tolerate conditions in most of the state—but you must pay attention to particular sites and microclimates for best results even with these hardy plants. An asterisk indicates a Montana native. For a more complete list, refer to *Tree and Shrub Selection Guide* and *Tree and Shrub Grower's Guide*, both from Montana State University Extension Service (see chapter 12).

Conifer Shrubs

Common juniper (*Juniperus communis*). Zone 1; 2 to 3 feet tall by 10 to 12 feet wide. Problems: winter burn, spider mite.

Creeping juniper (*Juniperus horizontalis*). Zone 2; 6 to 18 inches tall by 12 to 14 feet wide. Problems: winter burn, spider mites.

Dwarf mugo pine (*Pinus mugo* var. *mugo*). Zone 3; 8 feet tall by 8 feet wide. Problems: Becomes leggy, gets scale.

Savin juniper (*Juniperus sabina*). Zones 3 to 4; 4 to 6 feet tall by 12 to 14 feet wide. Problems: spider mites, twig blight.

Conifer Trees

American arborvitae (*Thuja occidentalis*). Zones 2 to 4; 1½ to 25 feet tall by 3 to 10 feet wide. Problems: winter burn; prefers cool conditions.

Black Hills spruce (*Picea glauca* var. *densata*). Zone 2; 30 feet tall by 15 to 20 feet wide. Problems: spider mite; slow growing.

Colorado blue spruce (*Picea pungens*). Zone 2; 100 feet tall by 25 feet wide. Problems: spider mite, spruce bud worm, cytospora canker; moderately difficult to transplant.

Douglas fir* (*Pseudotsuga menziesii*). Zone 4; 80 to 100 feet tall by 20 to 30 feet wide. For large landscapes; easy to transplant; best for elevations above 6,500 feet.

Engelmann spruce* (*Picea engelmannii*). Zone 2; 120 feet tall by 35 feet wide. Plant up to 9,500 feet elevation. Problems: Cooley spruce gall aphid; moderately difficult to transplant.

Ponderosa pine* (*Pinus ponderosa*). Zone 3; 60 to 70 feet tall by 40 to 50 feet wide. A Montana native. Problems: difficult to transplant; budworms.

Rocky Mountain juniper* (*Juniperus scopulorum*). Zone 3; 10 to 15 feet tall by 8 to 10 feet wide. Problems: spider mites, cedar apple rust.

White fir (*Abies concolor*). Zone 3; 50 to 65 feet tall by 15 to 20 feet wide. Problems: white pine weevil, spruce bud worm; moderately difficult to transplant.

White spruce* (*Picea glauca*). Zone 2; 50 feet tall by 15 to 20 feet wide. Problems: variable color and habit; moderately difficult to transplant.

Broadleaf Evergreen

Periwinkle (*Vinca minor*). Zone 4; 1 foot tall by 4 to 5 feet wide. Sun or shade.

Deciduous Shrubby Trees

Chokecherry (*Prunus virginiana*). Zone 2; 15 to 25 feet tall by 15 to 20 feet wide. Problems: suckers; black knot; moderately difficult to transplant.

Mayday tree (*Prunus padus* var. *commutata*). Zone 2; 15 to 20 feet tall by 12 to 15 feet wide. Does not sucker. Problems: black knot; moderately difficult to transplant.

Deciduous Shrubs

Alpine currant (*Ribes alpinum*). Zone 3; 4 to 6 feet by 6 to 7 feet wide. Good shade tolerance.

Amur maple (*Acer ginnala*). Zone 2; 15 to 20 feet tall by 15 to 20 feet wide. Problems: iron chlorosis; not for heavy soils.

Caragana (*Caragana arborescens*). Zone 2; 8 to 12 feet tall by 7 to 8 feet wide. Tolerates extreme drought. Problem: leggy.

Common lilac (*Syringa vulgaris*). Zones 2 to 3; 20 feet tall by 18 feet wide. Problem: suckers.

Hedge cotoneaster (*Cotoneaster lucidus, C. acutifolius*). Zones 2 to 3; 6 to 10 feet tall by 6 to 10 feet wide. Good hedge plant, takes shearing. Problems: pear slug, fireblight.

Korean barberry (*Berberis koreana*). Zone 4; 7 feet tall by 5 feet wide. Adapted to dryland sites.

Lewis mock orange* (*Philadelphus lewisii*). Zone 3; 4 to 5 feet tall by 3 feet wide. Cultivar 'Blizzard' is a profuse bloomer.

Red osier dogwood* (*Cornus sericea*). Zone 2; 5 to 10 tall by 6 to 7 feet wide. Problems: sprawls; winter burn; difficult to transplant.

Serviceberry (*Amelanchier alnifolia*). Zone 2; 6 to 8 feet tall by 5 to 6 feet wide. Problem: rust host.

Shrubby cinquefoil (*Pentaphylloides floribunda*, also known as *Potentilla fruticosa*). Zone 2; 2 to 4 feet tall by 3 to 5 feet wide. Long flowering season. Problem: mites.

Deciduous Trees

American linden (*Tilia americana*). Zone 3; 50 to 60 feet tall by 30 to 40 feet wide. Problems: weak wooded; moderately difficult to transplant.

'Autumn Blaze' maple (*Acer x freemanii*). Zone 3; 50 feet tall by 40 feet wide. Problems: leaf hoppers; borers.

Bur oak* (*Quercus macrocarpa*). Zone 3; 40 to 60 feet tall by 25 to 30 feet wide. Problem: difficult to transplant.

'Dolgo' crab apple (*Malus* cv. Dolgo). Zone 2; 20 to 25 feet tall by 16 to 18 feet wide. Problems: fireblight; moderately difficult to transplant.

Green ash* (*Fraxinus pennsylvanica* var. *lanceolata*). Zones 3 to 4; 50 to 60 feet tall by 30 to 35 feet wide. Drought and salinity tolerant; easy to transplant. Problem: borers.

'Morden' hawthorn (*Crataegus x mordenensis*). Zone 3; 12 to 15 feet tall by 10 to 12 feet wide. Cultivar: 'Toba'. Problems: pear slug; difficult to transplant.

Narrowleaf cottonwood* (*Populus angustifolia*). Deciduous tree. Zone 3; 50 to 60 feet tall by 40 to 50 feet wide. Tolerates high elevation planting. Problem: weak wooded.

Silver maple (*Acer saccharinum*). Zone 3; 85 feet tall by 45 feet wide. Easy to transplant. Problems: weak wood; iron chlorosis.

Deciduous Vines

'Dropmore' honeysuckle (*Lonicera x brownii* 'Dropmore Scarlet'). Zone 3. Problem: aphids.

Jackman clematis (*Clematis x jackmanii*). Zone 4. Dies back annually; blooms on new wood.

Virginia creeper (*Parthenocissus quinquefolia*). Zone 3. Problem: leafhoppers.

CHAPTER TEN

Native Plants

More and more new gardeners ask us to recommend some native plants for their landscape with the misunderstanding that any "native" plant will grow perfectly anywhere in the state, on any site, without water or fertilizer. That's absurd. All plants are native to somewhere, so when we talk about a native plant we have to define the area of its nativity. Is it native to Montana, the northern Rockies, the entire Rockies, the western United States, North America? Further, because we live in such a large state, all plants native even to Montana may not grow everywhere in the state. To find the native plant that is right for you, consider your location in the state and the site of the planting—wet area, benchland, and so on.

You must also accept that native shrubs will not have the same beauty as that lush rhododendron that was bred and selected especially for the landscape. Not all native grasses will be as dark green and fine textured as Kentucky bluegrass. Natives may be more hardy and tolerant of our conditions, but they are not "refined." But then, after all, the unrefined look does describe much of rugged Montana. If you accept this aesthetic and accept the limitations and requirements of native plants, then by all means use them in your landscape as accent plants to highlight a particular area of the landscape or as substitutes for less well-adapted plants more commonly planted.

Remember also that there are a great many plants that are well-adapted to our conditions that are not native to the state.

For example, common lilac (*Syringa vulgaris*), and caragana (*Caragana* spp.) do exceptionally well under our dry conditions, but neither is native to North America. Think long and hard about forsaking these fine plants simply because they are not native to Montana. Another mistake gardeners make is thinking that because a plant is drought tolerant it needs no water. Nothing could be further from the truth. The term "drought tolerant"

Finding Native Plants

"Native plants are popular with some Montana gardeners and landscapers because of the attraction of using plants well-adapted to our conditions," says Sharon Eversman of the Montana State University Ecology Department and a member of the Montana Native Plant Society. "Fortunately, many nurseries are carrying native flowers, shrubs, and trees that are well established in pots and can be planted directly into the garden or lawn.

"It is not considered ecologically sound to dig up native plants for transplanting," Eversman states. "Virtually all perennial native plants have mycorrhizal relationships with fungi," she explains. To transplant a wild plant, you have to dig up a huge soil mass around the roots to ensure you transfer the proper amounts of root mass and the symbiotic fungus. The resulting hole leaves a disturbed spot in a native community that makes weed invasion probable.

"It is more appropriate to collect mature seeds from native plants, generally sowing them in the fall so they have a winter stratification that allows germination," she says. "Most of the early growth is below ground, so it takes patience, and many years in some cases, to see above-ground growth and flowering. Thus, it is more advisable to take advantage of the nursery plants."

means only that it does not need as much water in quantity or frequency to remain functional. All young plants need water, especially before they become fully established, so don't plant caragana seedlings on a dry, windy bench with no provisions for watering them and expect them to thrive.

Once you have decided on the location of your planting, consider the actual site. Some native plants do well only under the shade of taller trees of a certain species, like Montana huckleberry (*Vaccinium* spp.). Others do well only when growing on streambanks or irrigation ditches, such as alder (*Alnus* spp.). Still others, like the mahonia (*Mahonia* spp.), require an acid soil or, like the bearberry (*Arctostaphylos uva-ursi*), a very well-drained soil with a good humus mat above. Yucca (*Yucca* spp.) does far better on very poor, dry soils than on rich, moist bottomlands. So again, just because a plant is native to Montana does not mean it will grow anywhere in the state under any condition. Match the plant to the location and the site.

When to Dig from the Wild

Generally, digging native plants from the wild may be illegal and is always cumbersome. However, sometimes the state will invite people to harvest wild plants in the interest of preserving them. "Exceptions to leaving native plants untouched have occurred when the forest service or other agency plans a road or construction where native plants will be disturbed," explains Sharon Eversman of MSU. In those cases, "members of the Montana Native Plant Society have been contacted with that information so that people can try digging and moving plants that may be destroyed anyway." For more information visit http://umt.edu/mnps.

Native Grasses

Many of these make fine ornamentals, reaching anywhere from 1 to 8 feet in height. Some are cool-season natives that thrive in spring and fall and brown out in summer. These include the Indian ricegrass (*Achnatherum hymenoides*), basin wildrye (*Leymus cinereus*), and bluebunch wheatgrass (*Pseudoroegneria spicata;* the official state grass of Montana). All are bunchgrasses and form attractive seed heads. All do well on loamy soils, though bluebunch wheatgrass and Indian ricegrass will also tolerate sandy soils. Native warm-season bunchgrasses include the big bluestem (*Andropogon gerardii*), little bluestem (*Schizachyrium scoparium*), and Indiangrass (*Sorghastrum nutans*). None of them are fussy about soils and all have attractive seed heads.

If it is a cool-season native lawn grass that you are after, consider western wheatgrass (*Pascopyrum smithii*) and streambank wheatgrass (*Elymus lanceolatus*). Neither is particular about soil and both are cool-season grasses that will give you a fair to good lawn. Warm-season native lawn grasses include blue grama (*Bouteloua gracilis*), buffalograss (*Buchloe dactyloides*), and sideoats grama (*Bouteloua curtipendula*). You can read more about native grasses for lawns in chapter 4.

Native Shrubs

There are a lot of shrubs native to Montana, but selection and evaluation work has been done on only a few. According to Mark Majerus and his associates at the USDA Natural Resources Conservation Service (NRCS) Bridger Plant Materials Center, most of these native shrubs have medium landscape value—that is, they would look okay in the right spot, but none of them are raving beauties. Following is a short list of some native shrubs commonly used in Montana home landscapes, including their *minimum* annual precipitation needs. More complete lists are available in MSU Extension Service Bulletin EB 162 and in the NRCS publication *Creating Native Landscapes in the Northern Great Plains and Rocky Mountains* by Majerus and colleagues.

American plum (*Prunus americana*). Zone 3. Partial to full sun; transplants easily in spring. Needs 14 inches precipitation.

Big sagebrush (*Artemisia tridentata*). Zone 3. Full sun; plant on dry, alkaline sites. Needs 8 inches precipitation.

Buffaloberry (*Shepherdia canadensis*). Zone 3. Partial to full sun; dioecious; transplants easily. Needs 14 inches precipitation.

Chokecherry (*Prunus virginiana*). Zone 2. Partial to full sun; transplants with moderate difficulty. Needs 12 inches precipitation.

Common juniper (*Juniperus communis*). Zone 2. Full sun; transplants best in autumn. Needs 12 inches precipitation.

Common snowberry (*Symphoricarpos albus*). Zone 3. Partial to full sun; transplants easily. Needs 14 inches precipitation.

Curlleaf mountain mahogany (*Cercocarpus ledifolius*). Zone 3. Partial to full sun; plant in fertile soil. Needs 10 inches precipitation.

Golden currant (*Ribes aureum*). Zone 2. Partial to full sun; transplants easily in autumn. Needs 12 inches precipitation.

Lewis mock orange (*Philadelphus lewisii*). Zone 3. Partial to full sun; transplants easily. Needs 15 inches precipitation.

Red osier dogwood (*Cornus sericea*). Zone 2. Partial to full sun; transplants easily. Needs much moisture.

Rocky Mountain juniper (*Juniperus scopulorum*). Zone 3. Full sun; transplants best in autumn. Needs 10 inches precipitation.

Serviceberry (*Amelanchier alnifolia*). Zone 4. Partial to full sun; transplants easily. Needs 12 inches precipitation.

Shrubby cinquefoil (*Pentaphylloides floribunda*). Zone 2. Partial to full sun; transplants easily. Needs 14 inches precipitation.

Skunkbush sumac (*Rhus trilobata*) Zone 3. Partial to full sun; transplants easily. Needs 10 inches precipitation.

Woods' rose (*Rosa woodsii*). Zone 2. Partial to full sun; transplants easily. Needs 12 inches precipitation.

Native Wildflowers

Everyone likes wildflowers, and Montana sure has its share of beautiful specimens. But not all wildflowers grow in all places. Some, like bitterroot (*Lewisia rediviva*), have special habitat requirements. Others, like littleleaf pussytoes (*Antennaria microphylla*), are short lived, while still others, like plains prickly pear (*Opuntia polyacantha*), have long life spans.

Because wildflower seeds are often small and hard to spread evenly, purchase small potted plants whenever possible. Prepare the bed as you would a lawn and plant in the cooler weather of spring and fall. As with other flowers, deadhead spent blooms to prolong the bloom season. Take care also to divide perennials regularly every few years to keep the plantings healthy and to give you the opportunity to improve the soil before replanting.

Wildflowers work well as specimen plantings, mass plantings, ground covers, and borders along your garden paths. But they must fit the overall scheme of the landscape. For example, if you have a proper, formal landscape, there is likely little room for wildflowers, which would fit better in a more natural landscape.

Here are some suggested native Montana wildflowers, drawn from *Creating Native Landscapes*, listed by the correct site/soil texture.

All Soil Types

American vetch (*Vicia americana*). Zones 3 to 5. Long-lived perennial; blue flowers. Full sun. Needs 10 inches precipitation.

Blanketflower (*Gaillardia aristata*). Zones 3 to 4. Long-lived perennial; yellow flowers. Full sun. Attracts butterflies; deer resistant. Needs 10 inches precipitation.

Common yarrow (*Achillea millefolium*). Zones 2 to 5. Long-lived perennial; white flowers. Partial shade to full sun. Deer resistant. Needs 9 inches precipitation.

Littleleaf pussytoes (*Antennaria microphylla*). Zones 2 to 4. Short-lived perennial; white flowers. Full sun. Needs 12 inches precipitation.

Lupine (*Lupinus* spp.). Zones 2 to 5. Long-lived perennial; flowers of all colors. Shade to full sun. Poisonous if ingested. Needs 14 inches precipitation.

Maximilian sunflower (*Helianthus maximiliani*). Zones 3 to 5. Short-lived perennial; yellow flowers. Full sun. Deer resistant. Needs 14 inches precipitation.

Plains prickly pear (*Opuntia polyacantha*). Zones 3 to 4. Long-lived perennial; yellow flowers. Full sun. Deer resistant. Needs 8 inches precipitation.

Prairie coneflower (*Ratibida columnifera*). Zones 3 to 4. Short-lived perennial; yellow flowers. Full sun. Attracts butterflies. Deer resistant. Needs 10 inches precipitation.

Smooth blue aster (*Aster leavis*). Zones 3 to 4. Moderately-lived perennial; blue flowers. Partial shade to full sun. Attracts butterflies. Deer resistant. Needs 12 inches precipitation.

Coarse and Medium Soil

Dotted gayfeather (*Liatris punctata*). Zones 3 to 4. Long-lived perennial; pink flowers. Full sun. Attracts butterflies. Deer resistant. Needs 10 inches precipitation.

Lewis flax (*Linum lewisii*). Zones 3 to 4. Short-lived perennial; blue flowers. Partial shade to full sun. Can become invasive. Needs 10 inches precipitation.

Spiny phlox (*Phlox hoodii*). Zones 3 to 4. Long-lived perennial; white flowers. Full sun. Deer resistant. Needs 10 inches precipitation.

Sticky geranium (*Geranium viscosissimum*). Zones 3 to 4. Long-lived perennial. Partial shade to full sun. Needs 14 inches precipitation.

Western pearly everlasting (*Anaphalis margaritacea*). Zones 3 to 4. Short-lived perennial; white flowers. Partial shade to full sun. Needs 10 inches precipitation.

White prairie clover (*Dalea candida*). Zones 3 to 4. Long-lived perennial; white flowers. Full sun. Attracts butterflies. Needs 12 inches precipitation.

Wooly cinquefoil (*Potentilla hippiana*). Zones 3 to 4. Short-lived perennial; yellow flowers. Full sun. Needs 14 inches precipitation.

Coarse Soil

Soapweed yucca (*Yucca glauca*). Zone 4. Long-lived perennial; white flowers. Full sun. Needs 8 inches precipitation.

Medium to Fine Soil

Blacksamson echinacea (*Echinacea angustifolia*). Zones 3 to 4. Long-lived perennial; pink flowers. Full sun. Attracts butterflies.

Deer resistent. Requires 12 inches precipitation.

Prairie thermopsis (*Thermopsis rhombifolia*). Zones 3 to 4. Long-lived perennial; yellow flowers. Full sun. Deer resistant. Needs 8 inches precipitation.

Native Trees

Some Montana native trees are prone to pest infestations and weak wood. Others are relatively pest free but take many years to make a beautiful specimen. With plenty of moisture pussy willows will grow to the roof every year if you cut them back hard and fertilize them, but they are weak and their growth unkempt. Bur oak and the green ash have strong wood but may take fifty years to become magnificent specimens. So plant a tree for your children to enjoy.

There are relatively few trees native to the state, and most of those are too big to fit easily and gracefully into most residential landscapes. Be sure you have the room if you want to plant a native tree in the backyard. On smaller residential lots it may be wiser to stick to planting a nonnative crab apple or a hawthorn.

All trees have problems you will have to live with. Aspens sucker. Box elders, actually maples, are weak wooded, and the female box elder attracts the box elder bug, which becomes a nuisance when the bugs congregate in your living room. Willows are weak-wooded water hogs prone to limb breakage and dropping shoots and twigs. So native trees may, or may not, have an advantage over adapted, nonnative trees. It's all in the mind of the beholder.

The following is a short list of trees native to Montana, including information about hardiness zones, mature height, areas in which they are native to Montana, and minimum annual precipitation requirements. For far more information than we can include here, consult MSU Extension Bulletins EB 123 and EB 162 (see chapter 12).

American elm (*Ulmus americana*). Zone 3; 65 feet. East; steambanks. Dutch elm disease has been identified in Montana; plant resistant cultivars only. Needs much moisture.

Box elder (*Acer negundo*). Zone 2; 55 feet. West, central, east; riverbanks, disturbed areas. Female trees attract box elder bug; weak wooded; adapted to tough conditions. Needs 12 inches precipitation.

Bur oak (*Quercus macrocarpa*). Zone 2; 50 feet. South-east; hills and canyons. Full sun; somewhat tolerant of saline soils. Needs 12 inches precipitation.

Engelmann spruce (*Picea engelmannii*). Zone 2; 120 feet. West, central; subalpine, slopes, moist woods. Subject to Cooley spruce gall aphid; too big for most landscapes. Needs much moisture.

Green ash (*Fraxinus pennsylvanica* var. *lanceolata*). Zone 3; 55 feet. Central and east; riverbanks. Reliable; moderately tolerant of saline soils. Needs 10 inches precipitation.

Ponderosa pine (*Pinus ponderosa*). Zone 3; 65 feet. All; foothills. Too large for most residential landscapes. Needs 12 inches precipitation.

Quaking aspen (*Populus tremuloides*). Zone 1; 35 feet. All; moist areas. Suckers badly; subject to borers; short lived. Needs much moisture.

Western hemlock (*Tsuga heterophylla*). Zone 5; 90 feet. Northwest; forests. Adapted only to northwest Montana. Needs damp environment.

White spruce (*Picea glauca*). Zone 2; 50 feet. Northwest, central; forests, swamps. Variable colors; hardy to most areas. Needs damp environment.

Willow (*Salix* spp.). Zone 2; 50 feet. Riverbanks; other wet areas. Weak-wooded, messy trees; subject to windthrow and borers. Needs much moisture.

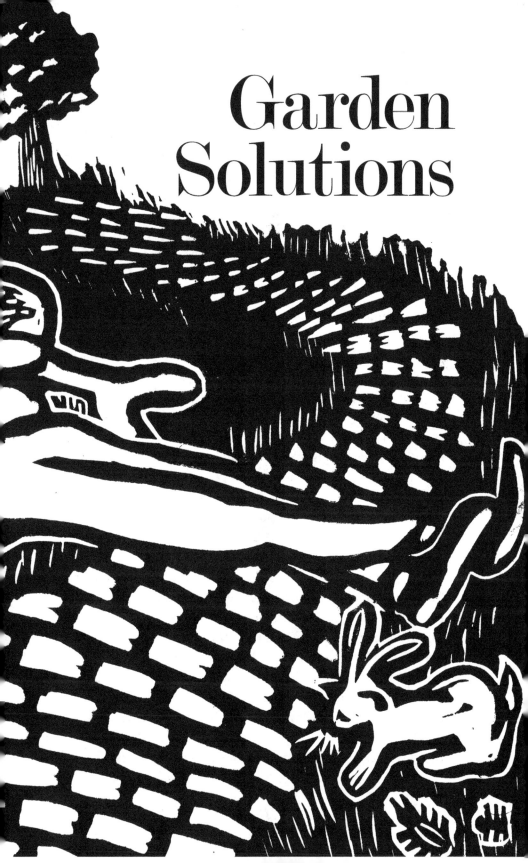

Garden
Solutions

Pests and Problems

Plant problems will always be with you. But there are some simple, commonsense steps you can take to help your plants stay healthy, because a strong, healthy plant will better resist problems that weak, stressed plants cannot.

- Be sure your soil has good drainage.
- Have an appropriate fertilization program. That does not mean giving plants high amounts of fertilizer. Think of your own nutritional needs. If eating 2,000 calories per day is just right for you, then eating 5,000 calories will get you into trouble. So too with plants. If two pounds of nitrogen per 100 square feet is recommended, applying five pounds of nitrogen will get your plants into big trouble. Soft, lush growth cannot stand up to pests and the environment. Plants that "struggle" a little bit— that is, that are not highly lush and soft—are usually hardier.
- Be sure you have planted the right plant on the right site. Planting a shade-loving annual in full sun on a southern exposure is a recipe for disaster, and planting a Zone 8 tree anywhere outside in Montana just plain won't work. Period!
- Control those weeds. They block sunlight and air circulation, compete with your garden plants for nutrients and water, and harbor insects and diseases that can jump to your flowers and vegetables.
- Begin with healthy plants of disease-resistant varieties. Planting

tomatoes that are genetically resistant to *Fusarium* and *Verticillium* will help tremendously where these soilborne diseases are present. Select fireblight-resistant apple varieties.

- Practice good sanitation in the yard and garden. Prune out diseased branches when you see them and clean up garden refuse as quickly as possible. A thorough cleanup in the fall is a must before the ground freezes.

- Always, especially in Montana, provide adequate water to keep plants growing nicely.

- Rotate vegetable crops. Practice a minimum three-year rotation in your garden if you can—that is, do not plant crops susceptible to the same pests in the same place for at least three years. Five-year rotations are better. For example, crucifers (such as broccoli, cauliflower, and cabbage) share a host of diseases and insects. Rotate so that no crucifer is planted where a crucifer grew previously for at least three years. Crop rotation also allows the crops to make the best use of nutrients in the soil.

If you think about it, all of these recommendations boil down to keeping the plant healthy and stressed as little as possible. A highly stressed plant is weak and less able to fend off attacks by insects and pathogens. In this sense, treat your plants as you should treat yourself.

Insects

There are far too many insect pests than we have space to discuss in this book, but a few are so common that we guarantee you will have to deal with them in your yard at some point. Some you can control by keeping the plant healthy or by using mechanical barriers, but you will have to rely upon using an insecticide to control others or where populations get out of control and cause unacceptable damage. What "unacceptable damage" is depends upon how you define it. If you are willing to live with a half-dozen worms in that apple, then you may not have to spray all season. If you can't live with more than one or two, then you will probably have to use control measures. If you won't accept *any* worms in your apples, then buy them at the local grocery! If a plant is completely defoliated through insect depredation, you waited too long to take action.

Use all methods of noninsecticidal insect control first. If they fail, then use an appropriate insecticide and *follow all label directions*. Not all insecticides control all insects, so you must know what insect is causing the damage in order to choose the best compound to control it. Be especially careful to apply just the right amount. The thought that if two tablespoons per gallon are recommended to kill the offenders, then four tablespoons per gallon will *really* kill them—well, that is irresponsible and downright stupid. Is "really dead" more dead than dead? Respect insecticides, but do not fear them. They are tools and they are no better and no worse than the person using them.

Systemic Pesticides

Systemic pesticides are applied as sprays or as granules sprinkled on the ground and absorbed by the plant. They enter the plant's water transport tissue and are moved throughout it, making all parts poisonous. They provide better protection than the older types of pesticides that remain on the surface of the plants in that they cannot be washed off and are able to protect parts of the plants that were not directly sprayed. However, for obvious reasons, you should not use systemic pesticides on edible crops.

Dormant Oil, Horticultural Oil, Insecticidal Soap

A dormant oil spray is a highly refined, horticultural oil spray applied when plants are dormant, usually in early spring. Horticultural oil is a highly refined 60-second or 70-second oil that is mainly used to control overwintering insects on woody plants. Insecticidal soap is a long-chain fatty acid soap used as an insecticide to control certain soft-bodied insects.

Following is a list of ten common insect pests that you will run into in our state.

Borers attack birch, pine, aspen, cottonwood, ash and many other woody plants, burrowing into the trunks and branches and interfering with the plants' ability to transport water and nutrients. If you see pencil-sized holes filled with what resembles sawdust and oozing a brownish liquid, your tree has borers. The first line of defense is to keep the plants healthy, but in cases of severe infestation, you will have to resort to using a systemic insecticide.

Grubs in the lawn eat the roots of the grass and are an invitation for skunks to prowl the area in search of an easy meal. When lawn damage becomes unacceptable, take care of the grubs with the right insecticide, usually one in granular form that is broadcast with a fertilizer spreader. Some brands may actually be mixed with fertilizer.

Flea beetles can devastate your potatoes, kale, cabbage, and tomatoes. They are far worse in some years. We know of no control for them once they become established other than to use an insecticide like rotenone or carbaryl when infestations are severe. Prevent early infestations by using a floating row cover made of a material such as Reemay or other spun or woven products.

Leaf miners seem always present in birch, columbine, spinach, chard, and beets. Usually the level of damage they inflict is acceptable without your having to resort to using insecticides. Trim off the infested vegetable leaves, eat the good leaves, and live with it.

Root maggots in radish, beets, and other root crops are difficult to control. They do seem to have a preference for radish, however, so planting those as a trap crop in the row of carrots and beets or in adjacent rows will draw the maggots away from the other crops. Long rotations of five years or more also work well where space is available.

Scales are tiny insects that suck the juices from leaves. They live beneath a waxy coating that makes it difficult for sprays to penetrate. If your mugo pine or other ornamental is heavily infested, you can use a surface insecticide when the scales enter their crawler stage about mid- to late May. Or you can apply a systemic insecticide or a dormant oil spray.

Thrips are difficult to control, as they live deep beneath flower petals or in the crown of the plant. They are terrible pests of gladiolus, roses, and onions. Use a systemic insecticide on roses.

There are several ways to control thrips on gladiolus. You can soak the corms for six hours before planting in a solution of four teaspoons of Lysol in one gallon of water. Plant immediately after soaking. Also, you can place one hundred corms in a paper bag with one ounce of naphthalene flakes (mothballs). Fold the top of the bag over and store the corms until spring planting. Lastly, storing the corms at 35 to 40 degrees Fahrenheit for at least four months will also kill the thrips. An old refrigerator should be ideal for this, so long as the corms don't freeze.

If your onions have thrips, clean the plot well at the end of the season and practice a three-year rotation.

Cutworms attack the stems at the soil line of newly transplanted tomatoes, peppers, crucifers, and the like. Use a tarpaper collar around the stems to block access to the worms. You can also sprinkle a little lime, diatomaceous earth, or wood ash around the stems to keep cutworms away, but be sure this material does not contact the plant stem.

Aphids are pests on just about all plants, sucking juice from the leaves and excreting a sticky substance called honeydew. The infestations on street trees in Miles City a few years ago prompted complaints from folks who were covered with the sticky fluid as they walked on sidewalks beneath the trees. Severe infestations debilitate the plant, and the black sooty mold fungus that grows on the honeydew gives the tree branches and trunks a sooty look. A steady stream of water from the hose will wash the aphids away. Repeat this every week, and take special care to hit the underside of the leaves where aphids congregate. Insecticidal soaps also control this pest. Since aphids and mites overwinter as eggs on tree trunks and branches, consider applying a dormant oil spray following years of especially heavy infestations.

Mites are particular problems on dense shrubs in hot, dusty locations. Junipers, cinquefoil, dwarf Alberta spruce, and roses are especially susceptible. The mites themselves are about the size of small pepper grains and infest the lower sides of the leaves, where they rasp away, rupturing the epidermis to suck the juices from the plants. Leaves infested with mites will have a silvery or gold speckled pattern to them. Because mites are more closely related to spiders than to insects, many insecticides are ineffective against them. As with aphids, a stream of cold water and/or insecticidal soaps sometime work, and application of dormant oil sprays is useful after years of especially heavy infestations.

Other insects, like tent caterpillars, beetles, sawfly larvae, and cabbage worms, are large enough to let you pick and destroy them manually. *Bacillus thuringiensis* is effective for control of cabbage worms and is approved for use in organic systems. You can easily burn tent caterpillars en mass if you thrust a lighted torch into the nest before the worms emerge. An old rag wrapped on the end of a stick and soaked in kerosene will answer the call nicely. These "mechanical" methods are always preferable to the use of pesticides and certainly let you get your hands dirty.

Disease Pathogens

Pathogens are agents that cause disease. Like insects, pathogens can overwinter in debris and infested stems. In autumn rake the fallen leaves and fruit from infected plants and remove them from the property. Likewise, prune out diseased shoots and branches and get them off location. Turn under uninfected and uninfested garden debris in your fall plowing and otherwise tidy up the yard and garden.

A pathogen cannot cause a disease on its own. It needs help. To cause a disease the pathogen must have a favorable environment *and* a susceptible host. The three components of a disease are the pathogen, the host, and the environment. Often called the "disease triangle," all three components must be present for the disease to occur.

Following are a half-dozen diseases that you will likely encounter in your Montana landscape.

Disease-Resistant Plants

"Gardeners in Montana must be aware of various plant diseases that can cause real problems for them," says Don Mathre, MSU plant pathology professor emeritus. "Purchase seed that has been treated with a fungicide to control seedling damping-off diseases. If you must use nontreated seed, be sure to wait until the soil has warmed enough to minimize damping-off.

"For other diseases that occur as the plant is growing, it is best to use disease-resistant varieties, especially tomatoes that are resistant to verticillium and fusarium wilt diseases," he advises. "Also, rotate your crops to minimize the buildup of pathogens in the soil. Because of our dry summer climate, we don't have much trouble with diseases that attack the foliage, with the exception of powdery mildew."

Not All Pathogens Are Equal

Pathogens may be viral, bacterial, or fungal. Sprays are available for the latter two, but the only means to control a viral disease is to rogue out the infected plant and practice good insect control. Insects are often carriers of viruses.

Fireblight is a bacterial disease that attacks apples, pears, cotoneaster, mountain ash, and some other members of the rose family. It is widespread in Montana, where infections begin with the first warm spring rains. Tissue infected with this bacteria looks like it has been burned black with a blowtorch, hence the name. New shoot growth that is blackened and bent like a shepherd's crook is the most common sign, but the bacteria can also blacken and blast flowers, cause mummified fruit, and cause cankers on branches and trunks.

To guard against fireblight, do not encourage soft growth by excess watering, excess nitrogen applications, or heavy pruning. Cut out all infected tissue in late fall or winter, making your cuts at least 10 inches below any signs of infection. Disinfect your pruning shears after every cut by dipping them into rubbing alcohol, Lysol, or a 1:9 mixture of household bleach and water.

Black knot is a fungal disease seen in the wild and in yards on *Prunus* species such as chokecherry, mayday tree, and plum. Fungal spores are produced during rains when the tree is in bloom or shortly thereafter. Long, black, corky knots form on branches, resembling a knotted black hot dog on a stick. The tissue distal (toward the tip of the branch) to the infection is killed when the knot girdles the branch.

Prune out knots 2 to 3 inches below the infection and remove the trimmings from your property. Disinfect shears between cuts.

Powdery mildew attacks many plants, including lilac, caragana, and Kentucky bluegrass. This fungus forms a white powdery film on the leaves that interferes with photosynthesis. In severe infections the leaves dry and fall, bringing photosynthesis to near zero. Promote good air circulation and sunlight penetration into the bush by judicious pruning and avoid wetting the foliage during irrigation. Usually fungicides are not needed.

Rusts are fungi that attack the leaves of a plant, usually causing bright orange- to rust-colored spots to appear. The tissue beneath these spots is damaged and photosynthesis reduced. Rusts are particularly common on roses and hollyhocks. As with all diseases, avoid wetting the plant foliage during irrigation and practice good sanitation, raking up and destroying all infected tissue in autumn.

A number of related rusts jump from junipers to a host in the rose family, such as apple, hawthorn, and serviceberry, causing cedar-apple rust, cedar-hawthorn rust, or cedar-serviceberry rust, depending upon which hosts are involved. These fungi must live part of their life cycle on the juniper and part on the other host. If one or the other is not present, the fungus dies out. The Bozeman area suffered a severe infestation of cedar-hawthorn rust in 2002 that devastated the wild hawthorn population. We clearly recall the hillsides turning golden in July with the infected hawthorn leaves.

Montana gardeners most commonly experience cedar-apple rust due to the presence of so many crab apples in our landscapes. The pathogen forms a hard, kidney-shaped gall on the junipers that swells into an orange, gelatinous mass with the warm rains of late May and June. This mass resembles a rusty-colored octopus and frightens children and novice gardeners. While it can kill small branches distal to the infection, it does not kill the plant. If it bothers you, clip it off and get it off your property. The pathogen shows up on apple trees as small orange spots on the leaves and fruit. No permanent harm is done to the tree, although the disease may cause defoliation in heavy infestations.

Cankers are caused by a number of fungi and bacteria and usually show up as dark-colored sunken areas on the trunks of trees or the canes of shrubs. Poplars, elms, spruce, and willows suffer from cytospora canker. This has been especially devastating on Colorado blue spruce in recent years. If you notice a dead branch in your spruce, examine it closely, looking for small amounts of whitened pitch that have oozed from the canker. There is no good control for cytospora canker other than pruning out the affected branches and canes. Nor is there good control for fireblight cankers, which appear as purplish or black areas on the trunks and branches of susceptible trees.

Many canker pathogens invade weakened plants through damaged areas of the bark. Plants that are constantly whipped by strong winds may develop small cracks at the soil line through which the pathogen enters.  Plants that have suffered sunscald often develop cankers around the affected tissue, and some canker pathogens enter plants through pruning wounds or trunks damaged by over aggressive lawn mowers. Keep plants healthy and reduce damage to a minimum.

Slime flux usually shows on elms in May and June, appearing as a leak of sap in a crotch or on the trunk. A bacterial infection causes the tree's sap to ferment. The gas pressure forces the foaming sap out of small cracks, from which it runs down the trunk to collect in a puddle at the tree's base. The foul brew smells sour and discolors the tree bark to a light tan. No plants grow where the sap collects. The old recommendation of boring and tapping the trunk is out of vogue. Trees do not often die of this infection, so simply leave them alone.

Fairy rings are caused by several soil fungi endemic to Montana. These fungi live on decaying organic matter buried in the soil, perhaps old tree roots or even building debris. The fungus begins at a point and moves out in all directions from the center, forming an ever-widening ring of foraging mycelia. The action is at the periphery of the ring, where the fungus actively breaks down the organic material and releases its stored nitrogen, some of which the fungus uses to sustain growth and some of which the lawn grass uses to sustain its growth. The grass greens where the nitrogen is plentiful, and the tell-tale "fairy ring" is formed. At times the fungal mycelial mat is so thick just back of the ring periphery that it blocks penetration of water and nutrients into the soil, killing the grass at that spot. Cool temperatures and moisture send the fungus into the reproductive stage and mushrooms form on the ring.

Fairy rings are unattractive and a nuisance, but there is no good "fairy-ring killer" on the market for homeowners. Instead, fertilize and irrigate your lawn to keep all grass looking as green as that in the ring, and give it a good core aeration every few years to punch through that mycelial mat. Otherwise, just live with the fairy rings. And don't eat the mushrooms unless they have been positively identified as being edible.

Dutch elm disease reared its ugly head in Montana during the summer of 2006 in Livingston. This disease is caused by the fungus *Ophiostoma novo-ulmi* and has decimated populations of American elm (*Ulmus americana*) throughout the United States. The fungus is spread from tree to tree by native and European elm bark beetles and to neighboring trees through root grafts. Homeowners who have American elm trees should look for wilting of the leaves on individual branches in the crown. Infected woody tissues will have a brown discoloration just under the bark. If you are concerned about an elm tree on your property, contact your local MSU county extension office for assistance.

Animal Pests

Montana is still a pretty wild part of the country, and some areas of the state are more wild than others. You may be able to fight insects and diseases pretty well, but four-legged critters will take every opportunity to use your yard and garden as a smorgasbord.

There are several pests that can run the gamut from being simple nuisances to doing real damage to your crops, according to Dr. James E. Knight, a wildlife specialist and associate director of the Montana State University Extension Service. Here are some common animals that can become problems for you. Learn all you can about them and learn how to control their predations. If you want more detailed information, see Knight's new book, *Manage Your Land for Wildlife.*

Raccoons are omnivores that can eat your fruit and vegetables but seem to be most destructive on sweet corn, the stalks of which they break before scratching away the corn husks to get at the sweet kernels for a mere bite or two. Planting squash around the corn can deter the animals sometimes, but dogs, pie tins, lights, and hard rock music are no deterrents at all. Since there are no registered repellants effective on raccoons, either live trap them, using a fish-based canned cat food for bait, or rig a single- or double-strand electric fence about 6 to 10 inches above the ground around your corn and melons. Put galvanized metal collars around your fruit trees to keep the raccoons out of them.

Skunks are carnivores that feed on mice and grubs. This is a good thing, though the 3- to 4-inch-deep cone-shaped holes they dig in your lawn in search of their meal make a real mess. The best way to handle skunks is to eliminate the grub problem in the lawn.

Bears will eat just about anything. They destroy corn and ravage fruit crops, breaking plant limbs as they go. They are tough to control. A four-wire electric fence about 36 inches high set to deliver a minimum of 4,000 volts is effective but expensive to maintain. Consider not planting fruit crops in bear country, and certainly do not use this electric fence with small children nearby.

Coyotes will also eat a lot of things. They are not a big pest in home gardens, but they will eat berries and low-hanging fruit. Dogs, llamas, and donkeys are effective deterrents.

Pocket gophers live most of their lives underground, plugging the holes to their tunnels as they go. They eat roots and tubers and present minor problems in most home landscapes. We had them in our onion patch one year. Frequent tillage, along with flooding the holes, got rid of them pretty fast.

Deer are the major pest of home landscapes in Montana. They eat fruit and berries and browse ornamental plants. If you live in deer country, plant deer-resistant plants adapted to your area, such as barberry (*Berberis* spp.), spruce (*Picea* spp.), honey locust (*Gleditsia tricanthos*), junipers (*Juniperus* spp.), pines (*Pinus* spp.), and lilac (*Syringa* spp.). Avoid great deer food like some firs (*Abies* spp.), winged euonymous (*Euonymus alatus*), apples, plum and cherry, American arborvitae (*Thuja occidentalis*), and hybrid tea roses. (Refer to MontGuide MT199521 AG, *Deer Resistant Ornamental Plants for Your Garden,* for more details.) We remind you, however, that the plants are deer *resistant,* not deer *immune;* deer will eat these plants too if they are hungry enough.

If you want to plant what you want to plant, and small children are not a concern, then put up a seven-wire electric fence starting about 8 inches off the ground and set to deliver about 4,000 volts on the charged wires. That is about all that will work. Frightening devices don't work and taste repellants are effective only until they are washed off the plants with irrigation or rain.

Rabbits are cute, furry little creatures until you see the destruction they can cause in your yard. Then they become fanged monsters. They can girdle trees in winter and eat your tender vegetables and landscape plants in the summer.

Rabbits are difficult to control unless you are willing to fence off their meals. Bury chicken wire 4 to 6 inches below the ground around your garden, leaving 1½ to 2 feet of fence above the ground. Where winter control is needed, be sure the fence reaches 2 feet above the snow level. Keep rabbits away from your trees in winter with a similar chicken wire cage 2 feet high around the trunk. Products containing thiram may be used on individual plants. Thiram tastes bad and thus deters nibbles, but it must be applied after each watering or rain. Blood meal is also reported to repel rabbits.

Voles are mouselike creatures that have a propensity to chew the bark off roots and the lower parts of tree trunks and shrub canes as they forage beneath the snow. The girdling damage often goes unnoticed until the plant wilts and dies with the advent of hot weather. Voles are particular pests of apple and crab apple trees and juniper bushes, but they can attack a large number of plants. They also are responsible for the tunnels in the lawn so highly visible just after snowmelt. Once the damage is done there is little you can do to "fix" it. Therefore, the key is prevention. Be sure to keep the grass mowed short, especially around trees and shrubs. Even better, place a stone mulch next to the trunks and out a couple of inches to reduce the cover for voles. Keeping a cat on the property doesn't hurt either.

Noxious Weeds

Eight-and-a-half million acres of Montana are covered with noxious weeds, decreasing the economic value of the land and crops, increasing soil erosion, and affecting the recreational value of the countryside. Farmers spend at least $100 million dollars in trying to control the weeds and in crop production losses. Some of these weeds enter the state on vehicles, on animals, or on the wind. Some even come into the state in wildflower mixes planted by innocent gardeners.

And as incredible as it may sound, some homeowners actually encourage noxious weed spread in the landscape because they think the plants look "pretty." We have a homeowner not too far from us who has a front lawn entirely covered with spotted knapweed. After repeatedly asking the owner to control the weed, the town "controlled" it for him, at the owner's expense. So be respectful of your neighbors and of our beautiful state. Do not spread these weeds deliberately, and make every effort to control them at their first appearance on your property. When in doubt about a weed's identity, contact your local county extension office or county weed board for help.

What is the difference between invasive plants and noxious weeds? "Invasive plants are those that displace more desired species and have the ability to dominate," explains Monica Pokorny, Montana State University research associate. "Noxious weeds are invasive plants that cause economic and/or environmental impacts and are a landowners' legal responsibility to control per the Montana County Noxious Weed Control Act. Noxious weeds are further defined by this act as being any exotic plant species that may render land unfit for agriculture, forestry, livestock, wildlife, or other beneficial uses or that may harm native plant communities.

"Plants can be designated statewide noxious weeds by rule of the Montana Department of Agriculture or countywide noxious weeds by district weed boards following public notice of intent and a public hearing. Currently, Montana has twenty-seven state-listed noxious weeds," Pokorny states.

Noxious weeds are grouped into three categories based upon the extent to which they have become established in the state. All noxious weeds are capable of spreading rapidly and rendering the land generally unfit for use.

Category 1: These are noxious weeds that are established and widespread in many Montana counties.

Whitetop complex (*Cardaria draba, C. pubescens, C. chalepensis*)

Diffuse knapweed (*Centaurea diffusa*)

Spotted knapweed (*Centaurea maculosa*)

Russian knapweed (*Centaurea repens*)

Oxeye daisy (*Chrysanthemum leucanthemum*)

Canada thistle (*Cirsium arvense*)

Field bindweed (*Convolvulus arvensis*)

Houndstongue (*Cynoglossum officinale*)

Leafy spurge (*Euphorbia esula*)

Saint John's-wort (*Hypericum perforatum*)

Dalmatian toadflax (*Linaria dalmatica*)

Yellow toadflax (*Linaria vulgaris*)

Sulfur cinquefoil (*Potentilla recta*)

Common tansy (*Tanacetum vulgare*)

Category 2: These have been recently introduced into the state or are rapidly spreading from their present sites. Again, they render the land generally unfit for use.

Orange hawkweed (*Hieracium aurantiacum*)

Meadow hawkweed complex (*Hieracium caespitosum, H. floribundum, H. piloselloides*)

Dyer's woad (*Isatis tinctoria*)

Perennial pepperweed (*Lepidium latifolium*)

Purple loosestrife (*Lythrum salicaria, L. virgatum,* and hybrids)

Tall buttercup (*Ranunculus acris*)

Tamarisk (salt cedar) (*Tamarix* spp.)

Category 3: These have not been detected in Montana or occur only in small infestations but are known to be pests in nearby states. As like the others, they render the land generally unfit.

Yellow star-thistle (*Centaurea solstitialis*)

Rush skeletonweed (*Chondrilla juncea*)

Common crupina (*Crupina vulgaris*)

Yellow flag iris (*Iris pseudacorus*)

Eurasian water milfoil (*Myriophyllum spicatum*)

Space does not allow us to give a lengthy discussion and description of each of these weeds, but you can get more information by getting a copy of *Montana's Noxious Weeds,* MSU Extension Bulletin EB 159.

Abiotic, or Environmental, Problems

Abiotic problems are those not caused by a biotic (living) agent. According to records kept at Montana State University's Schutter Plant Disease Diagnostic Laboratory, abiotic problems are by far the most common problems in Montana. Our intense sunlight, dry conditions, wind, and poor soil conspire to throw all sorts of challenges at our plants. The only way to deal with these problems is through prevention, for once you see them it's too late to take remedial action.

Windburn is just what it says—a burn or desiccation of the tissue caused by high winds. All plants lose water through their leaves and young shoots, and wind speeds the loss. When winds are excessive and the plants cannot replace the water loss due to drought, lack of irrigation, or frozen soil, then the leaves, needles, and small shoots will dry and die. The damage is most severe on the windward side of the tree. The needles of evergreens wind-burned in winter will turn a red brown as the temperature warms in spring. If the damage is not too severe, they will green again; if they brown and drop, you have probably lost the tree. For small trees, erect a wind barrier to help them survive. It's too late for large trees.

After the leaves on deciduous trees fall in autumn, water all trees and shrubs with about an inch of water per week until the ground freezes. This is especially important with evergreens. The fall watering will fill all internal reserves of the plant and allow it to go into the winter with its tanks full, so to speak.

Sunscald damage appears on the west or southwest sides of the trunks of dark-barked and young trees. In late winter the afternoon sun grows more intense as the trees begin to come out of rest and deharden. The cells beneath the bark respond to the warm afternoon temperatures but cannot reharden sufficiently to fend off the night cold after sunset. The result is dead cells. In mild cases the tissue sloughs off and the bark appears roughened in that area. In more severe cases all tissue down to the xylem is lost and the tree is disfigured. Often, canker-causing organisms enter through the wounds and the tree is lost.

Wrap the trunks of all newly planted trees for the first few years of their lives; wrap the trunks of all dark-barked trees, such as apple, cherry, and mountain ash, every year. Apply the tree wraps in October from the soil to the lowest branch and remove them in April each year. This wrap keeps the trunk cooler on late winter afternoons and reduces sunscald damage. You can also paint the trunks with white interior latex paint for good protection (do not use oil-based paint). Shrubs and evergreen trees need no protection from sunscald.

Scorch is a term that includes windburn, if it is caused by wind, but also applies to problems caused by excessive sun and heat. Like windburn, scorch is caused when the plant tissue loses water faster than it can be replaced. Plants on the south aspect lose water faster than plants on other aspects because of the warmer temperatures there. A plant next to the south side of a house is in a very warm spot. If the house is white or a light color, the reflection from it makes the problem worse. If that plant bed is mulched with crushed stone, which heats up, or is close to concrete or asphalt, the conditions may become unbearable and the plant scorches—that is, it toasts. When these conditions combine in winter when the soil is frozen, the plant very quickly uses all of its internal reserves of moisture, cannot replace that lost moisture, and dies. However, the death may not become apparent until the weather warms in spring, leading some to believe the plant died in June when it actually died in February.

Plants like raspberries may emerge from winter with the upper foot or so of the canes dead. This is the area of the cane most exposed to winter sun and wind. It also has a greater surface to volume ratio, which means it will dry out faster, and it loses its hardiness faster in early spring. For all of these reasons, the tops of raspberry canes regularly scorch. Fortunately the rest of the cane survives to provide you with plenty of fruit.

Overwatering is just as bad as underwatering and probably results in more plant deaths than the latter. Overwatering waterlogs the soil and fosters compaction, both of which lead to suffocation of plant roots. Saturated soil favors some grassy weeds in the lawn, such as roughstalk bluegrass, and restricts the growth of preferred grasses. It also encourages the growth of moss and algae. Overwatering puts more water onto the foliage and encourages foliar pathogens such as powdery mildew, fireblight, and black spot of roses. Who among us has not seen the ridiculous sight of lawn sprinklers going full force in a rainstorm, the result of some absent or absent-minded owner relying upon automatic timers instead of common sense? It is a squander of a valuable and scarce natural resource. Apply the right amount of water at the right time. More water than this applied more often is plain wrong.

Underwatering causes nearly as many problems as overwatering, but not quite. Sprinkling plants for five minutes with a hose does nothing but waste water. Be sure you water deeply and not too frequently (unless you are establishing a plant). Try to use drip irrigation and to otherwise apply the water to the soil and not to the foliage. We have seen so many people watering the foliage of a spruce in the misunderstanding that the tree absorbs significant amounts of water through the needles. A costly falsehood indeed!

Snow is a good insulator and protects plant roots from cold damage. But heavy wet snow, especially that of late spring storms after trees have foliated, cracks limbs, breaks canes, and splits trunks. Snow itself, being about 32 degrees, causes little cold damage to acclimated plants, but it can cause much mechanical damage. Brush it from the limbs as it accumulates and hope for the best. Protect plants beneath house eaves with an A-shaped tent formed from two pieces of plywood to shunt the snow to either side.

As the sun warms in late winter, snow develops an icy crust that can lead to suffocation of the plants beneath. Break that crust as it forms.

Ice is uniformly detrimental to plants. It has no insulation value and it suffocates plants beneath it. Ice is heavy as well; when it encrusts a plant, limbs and the treetop break. Ice that forms in an irrigation moat about the base of a tree can damage the tree's crown, allowing bacterial canker-causing organisms to enter as well as suffocating the roots. Where you can, remove ice as soon as it forms.

Hail causes significant mechanical damage in early summer, especially to large-leaved plants like rhubarb. However, it is rare that you get a complete loss of landscape and garden plants with the hail. Furthermore, there is little you can do ahead of time to prevent the damage. If you are home you might cover the plants with blankets, but often the damage is done before you can respond.

For more information on abiotic problems, consult the *Montana Master Gardener Handbook* (SR 100), a special publication of Montana State University Extension.

As in any other part of the country, plant diseases and environmental conditions can be tough on our garden plants. If you think you have a problem you cannot find the answer to, contact your local MSU Extension agent or any of the other applicable resources in chapter 12 of this book for assistance. Help is only a phone call away!

Resources for the Montana Gardener

We have referenced important information throughout the book. Use those references to gain information on specific items of interest. In this resource chapter you will find additional, general references that should be of great use to you in Montana gardening: Web sites and major works that will provide you with more information than space allows us to include in this book. You will also find contact information for MSU county extension offices. The agents in those offices provide nonbiased, science-based information on all aspects of agriculture and horticulture. Many varied questions will come up as you garden, and you will be forced to search for the answers. Don't be afraid to do so. Explore the wealth of information sources available to you. Use it all and use it frequently.

Master Gardener Program

The Montana Master Gardener program trains laypeople in introductory, general horticulture. The master gardener training policy is set by the national organization that oversees criteria for completion of the training. To become a certified Montana Master

Gardener, students must attend at least twenty-four hours of classroom training, successfully complete a comprehensive written examination, and satisfy a volunteer time requirement predetermined by the instructor and the student's MSU county agriculture agent involved in the training. Upon successful completion of all requirements, a master gardener certificate will be issued to the student. Each county decides whether to hold this twelve-week class, how much volunteer time is required (at least twenty hours) and how it is to be performed, and sets its own fees for the class. Some counties have offered multiple county programs, holding their classes in a convenient central location. The course's handbook has been written specifically for Montana horticulture and costs $35 as of this writing. You may order a copy of the handbook without taking the class by sending your check, payable to Master Gardener Account, to Cheryl Moore-Gough, Department of Plant Sciences and Plant Pathology, 324 Leon Johnson Hall, P.O. Box 173140, Montana State University, Bozeman, MT 59717. Your copy of the handbook will be sent immediately on receipt of payment.

Web Resources

http://gardenguide.montana.edu. This is the official extension horticulture site for Montana State University, and it's packed with valuable gardening information.

www.montana.edu/publications. This site provides information on the hundreds of publications of the Montana Extension Service. Or write to MSU Extension Publications, P.O. Box 172040, Bozeman, MT 59717-2040 for catalog information. We referenced these publications extensively for this book.

www.wrcc.dri.edu/climsum.html. This site provides current and historical information on Montana weather.

Print Publications

These are general and some specific gardening references that provide great information for the new or the experienced Montana gardener. Many are published by Montana State University, among them extension bulletins, MontGuides, and other brief, topic-specific publications, most of which are free for the asking. We list only a few; for a complete list contact the Montana Extension Service Publications Office.

Allison, E., and C. Jones. *Plant Water Relations.* Soil and Water Management Module 5. Montana State University Extension 4481-5, 2005.

Ball, J. *Rodale's Garden Problem Solver.* Rodale Press, 1988.

Caprio, J. M., and G. A. Nielsen. *Climate Atlas of Montana.* Montana State University Extension Bulletin EB 113, 1992.

Dinkins, C., and C. Jones. *Home Garden Soil Testing and Fertilizer Guidelines.* Montana State University Extension MontGuide MT200705AG, 2007.Gough, B., C. Moore-Gough, and L. Peters. *Best Garden Plants for Montana.* Lone Pine Publishing, 2005.

Gough, R. E. *A Montana Gardener's Book of Days.* Montana State University Extension Bulletin EB 165, 2004.

——. *Tree and Shrub Selection Guide.* Montana State University Extension Bulletin EB 123 rev., 2003.

——. "Color of Plastic Mulch Affects Lateral Root Development But Not Root System Architecture in Pepper," *HortScience* 36 (1): 66-68.

——. *Glossary of Vital Terms for the Home Gardener.* Food Products Press, 1993.

Gough, R. E., ed. *Montana Master Gardener Handbook,* third ed. Montana State University Extension Publication SR 100, 2004.

Gough, R. E., and T. Dougher. *Tree and Shrub Grower's Guide.* Montana State University Extension Bulletin EB 162, 2003.

Gough, R. E., and E. B. Poling, eds. *Small Fruits in the Home Garden.* Food Products Press, 1996.

Harris, R. W, J. R. Clark, and N. P. Matheny. *Arboriculture,* third ed. Prentice Hall, 1999.

Hollingsworth, C. S., ed. *Pacific Northwest Insect Management Handbook.* Oregon State University, 2007. Revised annually, this book is helpful for the advanced home gardener and horticulture professional. Get more details at http://pnwpest.org/pnw/insects.

Hortus Third. MacMillan, 1976.

Jones, C., and J. Jacobsen. *Micronutrients: Cycling, Testing and Fertilizer Recommendations.* Nutrient Management Module No. 7. Montana State University Extension 4449-7, 2003.

———. *Nitrogen Cycling, Testing and Fertilizer Recommendations.* Nutrient Management Module No. 3. Montana State University Extension 4449-3, 2005.

———. *Plant Nutrition and Soil Fertility.* Nutrient Management Module No. 2. Montana State University Extension 4449-2, 2005.

———. *Soil Sampling and Laboratory Selection.* Nutrient Management Module No. 1. Montana State University Extension 4449-1, 2005.

Knight, J. E. *Manage Your Land for Wildlife.* Montana State University Extension Publication, 2007.

Korb, N., C. Jones, and J. Jacobsen. *Secondary Macronutrients: Cycling, Testing and Fertilizer Recommendations.* Nutrient Management Module No. 6. Montana State University Extension 4449-6, 2005.

Majerus, M., C. Reynolds, J. Scianna, and S. Winslow. *Creating Native Landscapes in the Northern Great Plains and Rocky Mountains.* Natural Resources Conservation Service, Montana, 2005. This is a great publication that is useful for most of Montana.

McCauley, A., and C. Jones. *Salinity and Sodicity Management.* Soil and Water Management Module 2. Montana State University Extension 4481-2, 2005.

———. *Water and Solute Transport in Soils.* Soil and Water Management Module 4. Montana State University Extension 4481-4, 2005.

McCauley, A., C. Jones, and J. Jacobsen. *Basic Soil Properties.* Soil and Water Management Module 1. Montana State University Extension 4481-1, 2005.

———. *Commercial Fertilizers and Soil Amendments.* Nutrient Management Module No. 10. Montana State University Extension 4449-10, 2003.

———. *Soil pH and Organic Matter.* Nutrient Management Module No. 8. Montana State University Extension 4449-8, 2003.

Montagne, C., L. C. Munn, G. A. Nielsen, J. W. Rogers, H. E. Hunter. *Soils of Montana.* Montana State University Extension Bulletin EB 744, 1982.

Pscheidt, J. W., and C. M. Ocamb, eds. *Pacific Northwest Plant Disease Management Handbook.* Oregon State University, 2007. Revised annually, this book is helpful for the advanced home gardener and horticulture professional. Get details at http://plant-disease.ippc.orst.edu.

Smith, C., ed. *The Ortho Home Gardener's Problem Solver.* Ortho Books, 1993.

United States Department of Agriculture. *Yearbook of Agriculture.* 1941.

Water Management—The Montana Irrigator's Pocket Guide. National Center for Appropriate Technology, 2003. For details call (800) ASK-NCAT or visit www.ncat.org.

William, R. D, et al. *Pacific Northwest Weed Management Handbook.* Oregon State University, 2007. Revised annually, this book is helpful for the advanced home gardener and horticulture

Resources for the Montana Gardener   **189**

professional. Get details at http://pnwpest.org/pnw/weeds.

Wyman, D. *Wyman's Gardening Encyclopedia.* MacMillan, 1987.

Soil Survey Maps and Information

Contact the Montana state office of the Natural Resources
Conservation Service (NRCS) for soil survey maps of your county
and other soil-related information. The office is located in the
Federal Building Room 443, 10 East Babcock Street, Bozeman,
MT 59715-4704. Phone (406) 587-6811.

Soil Testing Laboratories in Montana

Montana State University no longer provides soil testing for
homeowners. Following is a list of private labs in Montana that
will test your soil for a fee. The authors do not recommend any
specific lab, and the list is not meant to be all-inclusive.

B&C Ag Consultants, 315 South Twenty-sixth Street, P.O.
Box 1184, Billings, MT 59107; (800) 764-1622, (406) 259-5779

Energy Laboratories, Inc., P.O. Box 30916, Billings, MT
59107; (800) 735-4489, (406) 252-6325

Maxim Technologies, Inc., 600 South Twenty-fifth Street,
P.O. Box 30615, Billings, MT 59107; (406) 248-9161

Montana Extension Service

Most of Montana's fifty-six counties have field offices with agents
ready to help you with all of your gardening questions. As you
will see, some offices serve two counties. In addition, American
Indian Reservations also have such service for gardeners located
on reservation lands. Feel free to contact the office in your county
or reservation for specific information related to your conditions.
This list was updated June 30, 2007.

Beaverhead County: 2 South Pacific, Dillon, MT 59725-2799; (406) 683-3785, (406) 683-3769; http://extn.msu.montana.edu/counties/beaverhead.htm

Big Horn County: 121 West Third Street, Room 101, P.O. Box 908, Hardin, MT 59034-0908; (406) 665-9770, (406) 665-9776; http://extn.msu.montana .edu/counties/bighorn.htm

Blackfeet Reservation: P.O. Box 850, Browning, MT 59417-0850; (406) 338-2650, (406) 338-3529; http://msuextension.org

Blaine County: 400 Ohio Street, P.O. Box 519, Chinook, MT 59523-0519; (406) 357-3200, (406) 357-2359, (406) 357-2199; http://extn.msu.montana.edu/counties/blaine.htm

Broadwater County: Courthouse, 515 Broadway, Townsend, MT 59644-1003; (406) 266-9242, (406) 266-3674; http://extn .msu.montana.edu/counties/broadwater.htm

Carbon County: 128 Main Street, P.O. Box 230, Joliet, MT 59041-0230; (406) 962-3522, (406) 962-3522; http://extn.msu .montana.edu/counties/carbon.htm

Cascade County: 1807 Third Street NW, Westgate Mall, Great Falls, MT 59404-1922; (406) 454-6980, (406) 454-6984; www.montana.edu/cascade

Chouteau County: 1308 Franklin Street, P.O. Box 459, Fort Benton, MT 59442-0459; (406) 622-3751, (406) 622-3012; http://extn.msu.montana.edu/counties/chouteau.htm

Custer County: Courthouse, 1010 Main Street, Miles City, MT 59301-3419; (406) 874-3370, (406) 874-3454; http://extn.msu .montana.edu/counties/custer.htm

Daniels County: 106 Railroad Avenue East, P.O. Box 187, Scobey, MT 59263-0187; (406) 487-2861, (406) 487-2699; http://extn.msu.montana.edu/counties/daniels.htm

Dawson County: 207 West Bell Street, Glendive, MT 59330-1616; (406) 377-4277, (406) 377-2022; www.dawsoncounty montana.org

Deer Lodge County: Courthouse, 800 South Main Street, Anaconda, MT 59711-2950; (406) 563-4035, (406) 563-4036,

(406) 563-4001; http://extn.msu.montana.edu/counties/deer lodge.htm

Fallon-Carter Counties: Courthouse, 10 West Fallon, P.O. Box 850, Baker, MT 59313-0850; (406) 778-7110, (406) 778-3431; http://falloncounty.net/extension

Fergus County: 712 West Main Street, Lewistown, MT 59457-2562; (406) 538-3919, (406) 538-7611, (406) 538-5144; www.tein.net/~msufergus

Flathead County: 800 South Main Street, Kalispell, MT 59901-5400; (406) 758-5553, (406) 758-5881; www.co.flathead .mt.us/4h

Flathead Reservation: P.O. Box 335, Pablo, MT 59855-0335; (406) 675-2700, (406) 675-2035; http://msu extension.org

Fort Belknap Reservation: RR 1 Box 66, Harlem, MT 59526-9705; (406) 353-2205, (406) 353-4153; http://msuextension.org

Fort Peck Reservation: Fort Peck Community College, P.O. Box 398, Poplar MT 59255; (406) 768-6330, (406) 768-6301; http://msuextension.org

Gallatin County: 201 West Madison, Suite 300, Belgrade, MT 59714; (406) 388-3213; www.gallatin.mt.gov/public_ documents/gallatincomt_ extension/extension

Garfield County: Courthouse, P.O. Box 81, Jordan, MT 59337-0081; (406) 557-2770, (406) 557-2567; www.midrivers .com/~garextn/

Glacier County: Courthouse Annex, 1210 East Main Street, Cut Bank, MT 59427-3152; (406) 873-2239, (406) 873-9103; http://extn.msu.montana.edu/counties/glacier.htm

Granite County: Courthouse, P.O. Box 665, Philipsburg, MT 59858-0665; (406) 859-3304, (406) 859-3771, (406) 859-3817

Hill County: 315 Fourth Street, Havre, MT 59501-3923; (406) 265-5481, (406) 265-5487; http://co.hill.mt.us/extension /index.htm

Judith Basin County: Courthouse, P.O. Box 427, Stanford,

MT 59479-0427; (406) 566-2277, (406) 566-2211; http://extn
.msu.montana.edu/counties/judithbasin.htm

Lake County: 300 Third
Avenue NW, Ronan, MT 59864-
2328; (406) 676-4271, (406) 676-
4272; http://extn.msu.montana
.edu/counties/lake.htm

Lewis & Clark County: 316
North Park, Helena, MT 59623;
(406) 447-8346, (406) 447-8347;
www.co.lewis-clark.mt.us/edu
cation/extension

Liberty County: 111 First
Street East, P.O. Box 607, Chester,
MT 59522-0607; (406) 759-5625,
(406) 759-5996; http://co.liberty
.mt.us/html/extension.html

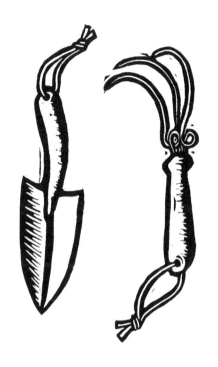

Lincoln County: 152 Highway
37, P.O. Box 1140, Eureka, MT
59917; (406) 296-9019, (406)
297-2767; www.lincolncountymt
.us/msu_extension.htm

Madison-Jefferson Counties: 309 East Legion, P.O. Box
1079, Whitehall, MT 59759-1079; (406) 287-3282, (406) 287-
3287; www.co.jefferson.mt.us/extension/extension.shtml

McCone County: 905 B Avenue, Vejtasa Building, P.O. Box
200, Circle, MT 59215-0200; (406) 485-2605, (406) 485-2306;
http://extn.msu.montana.edu/counties/mccone.htm

Meagher County: 15 West Main Street, White Sulphur
Springs, MT 59645; (406) 547-3612, (406) 547-3388; http://extn
.msu.montana.edu/counties/meagher.htm

Mineral County: 301 Second Avenue E, P.O. Box 730,
Superior, MT 59872-0730; (406) 822-3545, (406) 822-3840;
http://extn.msu.montana.edu/counties/mineral.htm

Missoula County: 2825 Santa Fe Court, Missoula, MT 59808; (406) 258-4200, (406) 258-3916; http://extn.msu.montana.edu /counties/missoula.htm

Musselshell-Golden Valley Counties: 116 First Street West, Roundup, MT 59072-2828; (406) 323-2704, (406) 323-1723

Northern Cheyenne Reservation: P.O. Box 128, Lame Deer, MT 59043-0128; (406) 477-6498, (406) 477-6488; http://msu extension.org

Park County: 414 East Callender Street, Livingston, MT 59047-2799; (406) 222-4156, (406) 222-4107; www.parkcounty .org/extension/extension.html

Phillips County: 10½ South Fourth East (Library Building), P.O. Box 430, Malta, MT 59538-0430; (406) 654-2543, (406) 654-2407; http://extn.msu.montana.edu/counties/phillips.htm

Pondera County: Courthouse, 20 Fourth Avenue SW, Conrad, MT 59425-2340; (406) 271-4054, (406) 271-4070; http://extn.msu.montana.edu/counties/pondera.htm

Powder River County: P.O. Box 269, Broadus, MT 59317-0269; (406) 436-2424, (406) 436-2482; http://extn.msu.montana .edu/counties/powderriver.htm

Powell County: Courthouse, 409 Missouri Avenue, Deer Lodge, MT 59722-1084; (406) 846-3680, (406) 846-2784; http://extn.msu.montana.edu/counties/powell.htm

Prairie County: 217 West Park Street, P.O. Box 7, Terry, MT 59349-0007; (406) 635-2121, (406) 635-5576; http://extn .msu.montana.edu/counties/prairie.htm

Ravalli County: 215 South Fourth Street, Suite G, Hamilton, MT 59840; (406) 375-6611, (406) 375-6606; www.co.ravalli .mt.us/county/extension.htm

Richland County: 123 West Main Street, Sidney, MT 59270-4129; (406) 433-1206, (406) 433-6885; www.richland.org /extension

Roosevelt County: 212 Broadway, County Building, P.O. Box 416, Culbertson, MT 59218-0416; (406) 787-5312, (406) 787-6612; www.montana.edu/roosevelt

Rosebud-Treasure Counties: Courthouse, Main Street, P.O. Box 65, Forsyth, MT 59327-0065; (406) 346-7320, (406) 346-7551; http://extn.msu.montana.edu/counties/rosetreasure.htm

Sanders County: 2504 Tradewinds Way, Suite 1B, Thompson Falls, MT 59873-0189; (406) 827-6934, (406) 827-4315; www.montana.edu/sanders

Sheridan County: Courthouse, 100 West Laurel Avenue, Plentywood, MT 59254-1619; (406) 765-3406, (406) 765-2129; http://extn.msu.montana.edu/counties/sheridan.htm

Silver Bow County: 305 West Mercury, #302, Butte, MT 59701-1659; (406) 723-0217, (406) 723-5345; http://extn.msu.montana.edu/counties/silverbow.htm

Stillwater County: Courthouse, 400 Third Avenue N, P.O. Box 807, Columbus, MT 59019-0807; (406) 322-8035, (406) 322-8007; www.co.stillwater.mt.us/extension/index.htm

Sweet Grass County: 515 Hooper Street, P.O. Box 640, Big Timber, MT 59011-0640; (406) 932-5146, (406) 932-5270; http://extn.msu.montana.edu/counties/sweetgrass.htm

Teton County: 1 South Main Avenue, P.O. Box 130, Choteau, MT 59422-0130; (406) 466-2491, (406) 466-2138; www.tetoncomt.org/extensionoffice/index.aspx

Toole County: 226 First Street South, Shelby, MT 59474-1920; (406) 424-8350, (406) 424-8301; http://extn.msu.montana.edu/counties/toole.htm

Valley County: 501 Court Square, Box 12, Glasgow, MT 59230-2423; (406) 228-6241, (406) 228-9027; http://extn.msu.montana.edu/counties/valley.htm

Wheatland County: 201 A Avenue NW, P.O. Box 733, Harlowton, MT 59036; (406) 632-4728, (406) 632-4880; http://extn.msu.montana.edu/counties/wheatland.htm

Wibaux County: 203 South Wibaux Street, P.O. Box 345, Wibaux, MT 59353-0345; (406) 796-2486, (406) 796-2625; http://extn.msu.montana.edu/counties/wibaux.htm

Yellowstone County: Courthouse, 217 North 27th Street,

Room 106, P.O. Box 35021, Billings, MT 59107-5021; (406) 256-2828, (406) 256-2825; www.co.yellowstone.mt.us/extension

MSU Extension Administrative Offices

Extension Publications: P.O. Box 172040, 115 Culbertson Hall, Bozeman, MT 59717-2040; (406) 994-3273, (406) 994-2050; www.montana.edu/wwwpub/expubs.html. Keep this address handy above all and use it frequently to order all of your Montana State University Extension publications.

Administration: P.O. Box 172230, Culbertson Hall, Bozeman, MT 59717-2230; (406) 994-1750, (406) 994-1756; http://extn.msu.montana.edu

Eastern Region Department Head: 243 Fort Keogh Road, Miles City, MT 59301; (406) 874-8236, (406) 951-0366

Central Region Department Head: 52583 U.S. Highway 87, Moccasin, MT 59462-9512; (406) 423-5421, (406) 366-2750

Western Region Department Head: P.O. Box 939, Polson, MT 59860; (406) 579-7694

MSU Extension Tribal Affiliates

Blackfeet Community College: Highways 2 and 89, P.O. Box 819, Browning, MT 59417; (406) 338-5441, (406) 338-3272; www.bfcc.org

Chief Dull Knife College: #1 College Drive, P.O. Box 98, Lame Deer, MT 59043; (406) 477-6215, (406) 477-6219; www.cdkc.edu

Fort Belknap College: Highways 2 and 66, P.O. Box 159, Harlem, MT 59526; (406) 353-2607, (406) 353-2898; www.fbcc.edu

Fort Peck Community College: Highway 2 East, P.O. Box 398, Poplar, MT 59255; (406) 768-6321, (406) 768-6301; www.fpcc.edu

Little Big Horn College: 1 Forestry Lane, P.O. Box 370, Crow Agency, MT 59022; (406) 638-3100, (406) 638-3169; www .lbhc.cc.mt.us

Salish Kootenai College: 52 South Highway 93, P.O. Box 117, Pablo, MT 59855; (406) 675-4800, (406) 675-4801; www .skc.edu

Stone Child College: R.R. 1 Box 1082, Box Elder, MT 59521; (406) 395-4875, (406) 395-4836; www.montana.edu/wwwscc

Glossary

abiotic: Nonliving. An abiotic problem is one caused by the environment and not by an insect or pathogen.

adventitious: Said of a shoot or root that arises from a bud that was newly formed in or near callus tissue as a result of removal of a large branch or of a serious wound. Shoots that arise from adventitious buds are highly vigorous and can restrict air circulation and sunlight penetration if allowed to develop. Adventitious roots are desirable in cutting propagation.

alkaline soil: A "basic" soil. A soil with a pH greater than 7.

allelopathy: A condition wherein one plant excretes substances that are toxic to certain other plants within the root zone or canopy of the first plant. Black walnut is perhaps the most famous example of this, the root exudates of which will kill tomatoes and apples.

annuals: Plants that complete their life cycles from seed to seed in one year.

biennials: Plants that complete their life cycles from seed to seed in two years. At the end of the first year, biennials usually form a clump of leaves on a very short, unnoticeable stem. This is called a rosette. In the second year a seed stalk emerges from the center of the rosette and the plant completes its life cycle. Dandelions are a good example of a biennial. Beets and parsnips are biennials grown as annuals.

brassicas: This general term refers to plants in the genus *Brassica*, which includes all of the crucifers. It is often used interchangeably with the term "crucifer."

broadleaf: A plant that has broad leaves as opposed to needles or grass blades.

buttoning: When the apex of cauliflower or cabbage is destroyed by insects or cold, the head will not form properly but will remain small and deformed. Hence, the plant is said to have "buttoned." This also occurs when seedling transplants are held in small pots too long.

C:N ratio: The proportion of carbon to nitrogen in a material. The higher the C:N ratio, the greater the amount of carbon, the longer it takes for the material to break down, and the more nitrogen microorganisms must use to accomplish that breakdown.

caliper: The diameter of a tree trunk.

cambium: A meristematic tissue in the plant that is responsible for producing an increase in girth. For example, the trunk of a tree becomes larger due to the activity of the cambium.

capillary water: Much of the water that remains in the small pores of the soil after gravitational water has drained. Most of this is readily available to the plant for absorption by the roots.

chinooks: Warm air masses that slide down the eastern slope of the Rocky Mountains in winter, resulting in a change in temperature of as much as 100 degrees Fahrenheit in twenty-four hours. The plummeting cold temperatures that follow often damage plants extensively.

chlorosis: A loss of green pigment (chlorophyll) caused by lack of light or by a nutrient deficiency. Interveinal chlorosis appears as a yellowing between the leaf veins while the veins themselves remain green.

conifer: A cone-bearing plant, such as a pine or spruce.

crucifer: A plant belonging to the Cruciferae, or Mustard, family. Broccoli, cabbage, cauliflower, brussels sprouts, and kale are some common crucifers.

cucurbits: Members of the Cucurbitaceae, or Squash, family. Melons, squash, cucumbers, and pumpkins all belong to this plant family.

deadhead: Removal of the spent flower to prevent the formation of seed and the accompanying drain of energy away from vital plant processes.

deciduous: A plant that looses its leaves in autumn. A few conifers, among them the larch, are deciduous.

dioecious: A plant type wherein the male and female flowers occur on separate plants. Some hollies, cottonwoods, and box elder are examples.

distal: A part of a plant more distant from the roots or trunk. For example, apple fruits are borne distal to the trunk or to the base of the branch to which they are attached.

double-worked: A tree is said to be double-worked if it has an interstock; that is, the tree was grafted twice, or "double-worked."

dripline: An imaginary line extending around the tree beneath the tips of the outer branches and that defines the periphery of the canopy.

epidermis: The outer "skin" of a leaf, shoot, or fruit.

ericaceous: A plant belonging to the family Ericaceae. Plants in this family generally do well in well-drained, low pH soil (about 5) with fairly high organic matter and in fairly humid growing conditions. Common ericaceous plants include the blueberry, rhododendron, azalea, mountain laurel, and cranberry.

etiolation: A physiological process brought about by insufficient light that causes plants to lose chlorophyll and to become soft and leggy. A good example is caused by a board placed on the lawn grass for a week or so and then removed. The grass beneath is yellowish and cannot photosynthesize properly. Plants cannot survive indefinitely in an etiolated condition.

evergreen: A plant that does not drop all of its leaves at once but over a number of years, so that its general appearance is always green. Most conifers, rhododendrons, bearberry, and laurel are evergreens.

field capacity: Soil is said to be at field capacity when it holds as much water as it can against the force of gravity. For example, after gravitational water has drained from the soil, the soil is then at field capacity.

frost crack: A vertical crack along the trunk of a tree caused by extreme cold in the vicinity of minus 25 to minus 30 degrees. The crack usually closes when the temperature warms and will heal in a few years. Frost cracks are also called "vertical shakes" and "trunk split."

girdling: Damage that encircles the trunk of a tree or cane of a shrub, severing the phloem and perhaps damaging the cambium. Complete girdling kills the plant.

gravitational water: Water in a saturated soil that is drained by the force of gravity alone. Hold saturated soil in your hand without squeezing it. The water that runs from the soil through your fingers is gravitational water.

gray water: Water used for washing laundry and kitchen utensils.

graft union: The point of attachment of the stock and the scion.

green manure: A cover crop that is turned under to build the soil is said to be a green manure crop.

half-hardy: This term is usually applied to annuals or vegetables that will tolerate some degree of cold. Half-hardy transplants can be set out a couple of weeks before the last frost, if well hardened.

harden: The ability of a plant to "toughen up" and survive harsh conditions, usually in terms of winter cold and desiccation.

hardiness zones: There are several systems of hardiness zones, the most famous of which is the United States Department of Agriculture's Zone Map of 1990. In this system North America is divided into 11 zones based upon average minimum winter temperatures. Zone 1 is in the far north, Zone 11 in Key West, Florida. Most of the continental United States lies in Zones 3 through 10. Zones 3, 4, and 5 cover most of Montana. There are some areas of Zone 2 in the highest mountains of the state.

hardy: In general terms, used to define a plant that will tolerate hard freezes, the degree to which depends upon the plant species. For example, a hardy vegetable may tolerate temperatures of about 25 degrees if well hardened, while a hardy tree, such as apple, may tolerate temperatures of minus 40. In specific terms, the word may be modified to refer to a plant that is "heat hardy," "wind hardy," etc.

hips: The fruit of the rose plant.

incipient wilt: That point when soil has reached about 60 to 50 percent of field capacity. The remaining water is held tightly enough that it becomes limiting during stressful times of the day. As a result, plants, particularly those with large leaves like squash and cucumbers, wilt. They recover at night only to wilt once more the following day unless water is applied. Without irrigation a state of incipient wilt quickly becomes one of permanent wilt.

interstock: In grafting, a piece of wood inserted into the rootstock. The scion is inserted into the interstock, giving three distinct types of wood to the tree. The interstock can be used to produce a dwarfing effect or to increase hardiness and disease resistance in the trunk of the future tree.

macronutrient: One of nine essential plant nutrients used in relatively large quantities by the plants. These include nitrogen, phosphorus, potassium, calcium, magnesium, and sulfur. The remaining three—oxygen, hydrogen, and carbon—are present in air and water and therefore never deficient.

microclimate: The climatic conditions found on a small scale around the yard. For example, the north and south sides of your house have different microclimates. A tomato plant covered with a Hot Kap in spring has a different microclimate from one not covered.

micronutrient: One of several essential plant nutrients used in relatively small quantities by the plants. These include iron, manganese, zinc, copper, molybdenum, boron, nickel, and cobalt.

monoecious: A perfect-flowered plant or a plant type wherein the male and female flowers occur on the same plant. That is, both sexes are on the same plant. Tomatoes, corn, and gladiolus are examples.

mycelia: The network of fine filaments (hyphae) of a fungus.

peds: Soil aggregates.

perennials: Plants that live for many years, usually setting seeds at the end of each season. Trees and shrubs are woody perennials. Herbaceous perennials, such as iris and narcissus, have tender aboveground parts that die back every fall, but the roots continue to live for many years, producing a new top each year.

permanent wilting point: That point at which all plant-available water has been extracted from the soil, forcing the plant to wilt, a state from which it will not recover.

pH: In agriculture, a logarithmic scale of 1 to 14 that expresses the relative proportions of hydrogen ions to hydroxyl ions. When the amounts of each ion balance, the soil is said to be neutral and the pH is 7. As the pH decreases from neutral, the soil becomes increasingly acid; as it increases, it becomes increasingly alkaline. Most garden plants do best when the pH is slightly acid. Most soils in Montana have slightly to decidedly alkaline pH.

phloem: A conducting tissue toward the outside of a stem, just beneath the bark or epidermis, that is responsible primarily for the transport of carbohydrates manufactured in the leaves to lower portions of the plant, including the roots.

phytotoxicity: Literally, "toxic to the plant." Some pesticides may be phytotoxic, that is, may damage the fruit or foliage of the plant.

plant available water (PAW): The soil water that is available to the plant; that is, the water that is present when the soil is between field capacity and the permanent wilting point.

rhizomes: Underground shoots by which some plants reproduce vegetatively. These are found in many plants, including raspberries and quackgrass.

rosette: A cluster of leaves resulting from the first-year growth of a biennial. In the second year a flower stalk emerges from the rosette center. The cluster of leaves of the beet, spinach, and dandelion typify a rosette.

rootstock: In grafting, the portion bearing the root system into which the piece of wood of the variety to be propagated (scion) is inserted.

saline soil: Soil with a high salt content.

scion: In grafting, the piece of wood or bud that is to be propagated by insertion into a stock.

self-fruitful: Said of a plant that will reproduce a good crop of fruit by its own pollen.

self-unfruitful: Said of a plant that will not reproduce a good crop of fruit by its own pollen.

shrub: A woody perennial with many trunks, sometimes called canes, by which the plant continuously rejuvenates itself. Common shrubs include lilac, mock orange, and spirea.

sodic soil: Soil with high sodium content.

stolons: Modified aboveground shoots by which some plants reproduce vegetatively. These are the "runners" in strawberries.

systemic: A compound, such as an insecticide or fungicide, which enters into the water-conducting system of the plant and is transported throughout all tissues, rendering them toxic to the pest. Never use a systemic on an edible crop.

strain: In fruit and vegetables, variations of a cultivar with valued characteristics. The variation is not great enough to warrant a new cultivar name but it is valuable enough to warrant propagation. For example, 'Red McIntosh' is a strain of 'McIntosh' that produces fruit redder than the parent strain, but they are still 'McIntosh' and possess all other 'McIntosh' traits.

sucker: A vigorous shoot that arises from below the soil line of a plant. In trees like aspen this is undesirable, but in shrubs it is a means for propagation and rejuvenation of the plant.

sunscald: A physiological disorder usually caused by intense late winter sun warming the south and west sides of deciduous trees. The tissue beneath the bark is killed and may slough off, leaving an entrance for canker and other pathogens. This is a major problem on trees with dark-colored bark and on young trees.

tender: This term is usually applied to vegetables and annuals that tolerate very little to no cold. Tender plants can be set out about the average date of last frost, if hardened properly.

tip layer: A method of vegetative propagation whereby the tip of a young shoot bends or is bent to the ground. It roots in contact with the soil, producing a new, "daughter" plant. Some plants like gooseberry and grape readily tip layer naturally.

tree: A woody perennial with a single stem (trunk), such as an ash or an oak tree. Some trees sucker profusely, like chokecherry, and unless the suckers are removed the tree may become shrubby.

very tender: This is said of vegetables and annuals that not only will tolerate no cold but should not be planted outdoors until the soil has warmed to about 70 degrees, or about two to three weeks after the average date of last frost. These plants cannot be hardened, and the very process of hardening them may destroy them.

watersprout: A vigorous, upright shoot arising from an aboveground portion of the woody plant. These are generally undesirable and should be removed immediately in most cases.

wind throw: The blowing over of shallow-rooted trees in a wind storm. Often encountered with willows.

xylem: A plant conducting tissue usually located near the interior of the trunk or stem that is primarily responsible for movement of water and nutrients from the soil to the upper portions of the plant.

Index

A

abiotic problems, 180–84
acid soils, 13
alkaline soils, 12
alliums, 91
annuals, 112–19
    half-hardy, 112
    hardy, 112
    maintenance, 116
    planting, 115–16
    selection, 112, 116–19
    tender, 112
    transplanting, 113–16
aphids, 169
apples, 95, 96, 97, 99, 101–2
apricots, 94, 95, 96, 103
asparagus, 76, 79, 85, 93

B

beans, 73, 76, 77, 79, 81, 87,
    89, 93
bears, 98, 104, 176
beets, 76, 77, 79, 81, 82, 87
biennial flowers, 121
birds, 98, 104
blackberries, 94,110
black knot, 171
blueberries, 94, 96
bonemeal, 127
borers, 167
boron, 15
broccoli, 74, 79, 81, 82

brussels sprouts, 73, 82
buffaloberries, 94, 110–11
bulbs, 126–29
    care, 127
    planting, 126–27
    selection, 128–29
    transplanting, 127–28
bush fruit, 94

C

cabbage, 74, 76, 79, 81, 82
calcium, 20
calendar, garden, 39–41
cankers, 172–73
carrot, 73, 76, 77, 79, 81, 87,
    93
cauliflower, 73, 76, 79, 82
celery, 82
chard, 73, 79, 82
cherries
    bush, 94, 105, 106
    sour, 94, 96, 104
    sweet, 94, 97, 104
chinooks, 29
chives, 76, 91
chlorine, 22
climate, 29–42
    chinooks, 29
    frost dates, 33, 36
    garden calendar, 39–41
    growing season, 30–35
    hardiness zones, 30, 31

microclimates, 31–32, 37–39
precipitation, 35–36
C:N ratio, 5–6
compost, 8–10
copper, 21–22
corn, 73, 76, 77, 79, 81, 82, 85, 89, 91–92
cover crop, 7–8
coyotes, 176
cranberries, 96
crop rotation, 77–78
cucumber, 73, 76, 79, 81, 82, 85, 87, 92
cucurbits, 92–93
currants, 94, 95, 99, 106, 107–8
cutworms, 168

D
deer, 176–77
disease control, 97, 170–75
dog urine, 71
drought-tolerant plants, 52–53
Dutch elm disease, 175

E
eggplant, 73, 74, 76, 81, 82

F
fairy rings, 68–69, 173–74
fertility, 18–22
fertilizers, 23–28
fertilizing, 99, 122, 141–42
field capacity, 45

fireblight, 97, 171
flea beetle, 167
frost cracks, 103, 104
frost dates, 33, 36
fruit, 94–111
apples, 95, 96, 97, 99, 101–2
apricots, 94, 95, 96, 103
bears, 98
birds, 98
blackberries, 94, 110
blueberries, 94, 96
buffaloberries, 94, 110–11
bush, 94
cherries, 94, 96, 97, 104, 105, 106
cranberries, 96
currants, 94, 95, 99, 106, 107–8
diseases, 97
fertilizing, 99
fireblight, 97
first fruit, 95
gooseberries, 94, 95, 99, 106, 107–8
grapes, 94, 95, 97, 99, 106, 108–9
insects, 97–98
lingonberries, 96
mulberries, 96
nuts, 96, 105–106
pears, 94, 97, 99, 102–3
planting, 98
pollination, 96

purchasing, 98
serviceberries, 94, 110–11
small fruit, 106–11
soil pH, 96
strawberries, 94, 95, 97, 99,
    107, 109
sunscald, 97, 104, 105
tree fruit, 99–106

G
gardening resources, 185–97
garlic, 91
gooseberries, 94, 95, 99, 106,
    107–8
grasses, native, 154–55
grapes, 94, 95, 97, 99, 106,
    108–9
green manure, 7
growing season, 30–35
grubs, 167
gumbo soil, 3
gypsum, 14–15

H
hail, 184
hardiness zones, 30–31
heirloom vegetables, 81–82
herbaceous perennials, 120–25
    care, 122–23
    defined, 120–21
    selection, 123–25
    soil, 121–22
    and wildlife attraction, 121

I
ice, 183
incipient wilt, 46
insects, 70, 97–98, 165–69
iron, 21

K
kale, 81, 93
kohlrabi, 87

L
lawns, 56–71
    cool-season, 57–60
    disease control, 68–69
    dog urine, 71
    establishment, 62–64
    fairy rings, 68–69
    grass blends, 56–61
    insects, 70
    maintenance, 65–68
    snow mold, 67, 69
    species, 61
    thatch, 59, 67
    tree wells, 62
    warm-season, 60–61
    weed control, 70
leach fields, 145
leaf miners, 167–168
legumes, 93
lettuce, 73, 76, 77, 79, 81,
    82, 87
lingonberry, 96

M

magnesium, 20
manure, 8
manganese, 22
Master Gardener program,
    Montana, 185–86
microclimates, 31–32, 37–39
mites, 169
molybdenum, 22
mulberries, 96
mulches, 50–52
muskmelon, 73, 74, 76, 81, 82,
    85, 87, 92

N

native plants, 151–61
    defined, 151
    grasses, 154–55
    planting, 153
    shrubs, 155–56
    trees, 159–61
    wildflowers, 156–59
nickel, 22
nitrogen, 19
nurse planting, 84
nuts, 96, 105–6

O

onion, 73, 76, 77, 81, 82,
    89, 91
organic matter, 5–10
overwatering, 182–83

P

parsnips, 76, 93
peaches, 94, 95, 103
pears, 94, 97, 99, 102–3
peas, 73, 76, 77, 79, 81, 87,
    89, 93
peppers, 73, 74, 76, 77, 79,
    81, 82
permanent wilt, 46
pests and problems, 164–84
    abiotic, 180–84
    animal, 175–78
    control (general), 164–65
    diseases, 170–75
    insects, 165–69
    weeds, 178–80
pH (soil), 96, 10–12
phosphorus, 19–20
plant-available water, 46
plums, 95, 104–5
pollination (fruit), 96
potassium, 20
potato, 76, 77, 81
precipitation, 35–36
powdery mildew, 171–72
pumpkin, 73, 76, 81, 92

R

rabbits, 177
raccoons, 175–76
radish, 73, 76, 79
raspberries, 94, 95, 96, 97,
    107, 110
rhubarb, 85, 88, 93

root maggots, 168
roses, 130–34
    care, 132–33
    planting, 131–32
    selection, 130–31, 134
rust, 172
rutabaga, 76

S
salt-tolerant plants, 15–18
salty soil, 13–18
scales, 168
scorch, 182
serviceberries, 94, 110–11
shrubs, native, 155–56
skunks, 176
slime flux, 173
small fruit, 94, 106–11
snow, 183
snow mold, 67, 69
soil, 2–28
    alkaline, 12
    acid, 13
    boron toxicity, 15
    chemical properties, 10–18
    C:N ratio, 5–6
    compost, 8–10
    cover crops, 7–8
    fertility, 18–22
    fertilizers, 23–28
    green manure, 7
    gumbo, 3
    gypsum, 14–15
    ideal, 2

manure, 8
nutrients, 19–22
organic matter, 5–10
pH, 10–12
salty, 13–18
salt-tolerant plants, 15–18
structure, 4–5
test, 22–23, 190
texture, 3–4
types, 2–3
soil amendments, 76–78, 91
soybeans, 77
spinach, 73, 76, 82, 93
squash, 73, 74, 76, 77, 79, 81,
    82, 87, 89, 92
strawberries, 94, 95, 97, 99,
    107, 109
sulfur, 20–21
sunscald, 97, 104, 105, 181–82

T
thatch, 59, 67
thrips, 168
tomato, 73, 74, 76, 77, 79, 82,
    87, 93
tree fruit, 99–106
trees and shrubs, 135–50
    fertilizing, 141–42
    leach fields, 145
    planting, 138–41
    pruning, 143–45
    purchasing, 136–38
    recommended species,
        147–50

selection, 135
transplanting, 136
troublesome species, 145–47
watering, 142
tree wells, 62

U
underwatering, 183

V
vegetables, 72–93
asparagus, 76, 79, 85, 93
beans, 73, 76, 77, 79, 81,
  87, 89, 93
beets, 77, 79, 81, 82, 87
broccoli, 74, 79, 81, 82
brussels sprouts, 73, 82
cabbage, 74, 76, 79, 81, 82
carrot, 73, 76, 77, 79, 81,
  87, 93
cauliflower, 73, 76, 79, 82
celery, 82
chard, 73, 79, 82
chives, 76, 91
corn, 73, 76, 77, 79, 81, 82,
  85, 89, 91–92
crop rotation, 77–78
cucumber, 73, 76, 79, 81, 82,
  85, 87, 92
days to maturity, 73
direct sowing, 84–85
eggplant, 73, 74, 76, 81, 82
garlic, 91
heirloom seeds, 81–82

kale, 81, 93
kohlrabi, 87
lettuce, 73, 76, 77, 79, 81,
  82, 87
muskmelon, 73, 74, 76, 81,
  82, 85, 87, 92
nurse crops, 84
onion, 73, 76, 77, 81, 82,
  89, 91
parsnips, 76, 93
peas, 73, 76, 77, 79, 81, 87,
  89, 93
peppers, 73, 74, 76, 77, 79,
  81, 82
perennials, 85–86
pH, 76
planning the garden, 72–76
potato, 76, 77, 81
preserving, 75
pumpkin, 73, 76, 81, 92
radish, 73, 76, 79
raised beds, 86–87
rhubarb, 85, 88, 93
rutabaga, 76
season extension, 90–91
seed selection, 78–80
soil amendments, 76–78, 91
soybeans, 77
special notes, 91–93
spinach, 73, 76, 82, 93
squash, 73, 74, 76, 77, 79,
  81, 82, 87, 89, 92
tomato, 73, 74, 76, 77, 79,
  82, 87, 93

transplants, 82–84
urban/intensive gardening,
    86–87
watering, 87–89
watermelon, 76, 82, 85, 92
weeds, 89
voles, 177–78

W
water relations, 42–53
conservation, 49–53
drought-tolerant plants,
    52–53
field capacity, 45
incipient wilt, 46
mulches, 50–52
permanent wilt, 46
plant-available water, 46
plant use, 42–45
watering, 45–49
watermelon, 76, 82, 85, 92
weeds, 70, 89
wildflowers, native, 156–59
windburn, 181

Z
zinc, 21

About the Authors

Bob Gough, PhD, is professor of horticulture and associate dean for academic programs in the College of Agriculture at Montana State University. A former editor of several scientific journals and books and the author of nine gardening books, more than five hundred extension services publications, and articles in such gardening magazines as *Fine Gardening, National Gardening, Harrowsmith,* and *Country Journal,* he founded and was the regular host of the *Northern Garden Tips* radio show for eight years. "Dr. Bob," as he is known throughout the state, is a Fellow of the American Society for Horticultural Science and a Teaching Fellow of the North American Colleges and Teachers of Agriculture.

Cheryl Moore-Gough, MS, is the Montana State University Extension state horticulturist and the Montana Master Gardener program coordinator. She has authored more than fifteen extension service publications, regular biweekly columns that appear in forty area newspapers, and articles for *Fine Gardening, American Nurseryman,* and *Montana Magazine.* She is the present host of *Northern Garden Tips.* This is her second gardening book. When not involved in gardening, Cheryl trains in and teaches the Japanese martial art of aikido. She holds the rank of sandan, or third-degree black belt.

Both authors make regular appearances on PBS's *Montana Ag Live* television show.

CPSIA information can be obtained
at www.ICGtesting.com
Printed in the USA
BVHW081409130521
607269BV00011B/1998